ULTIMATE COMICS
HAWKEYE

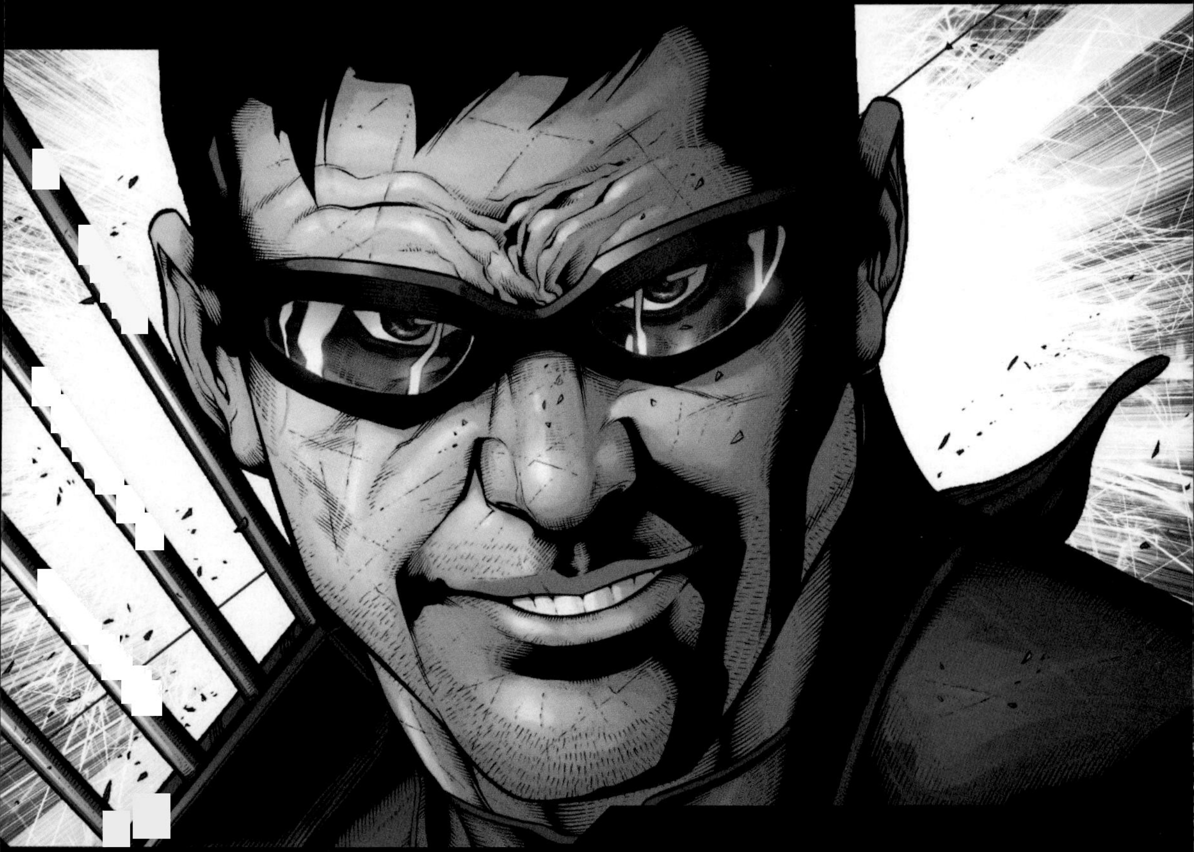

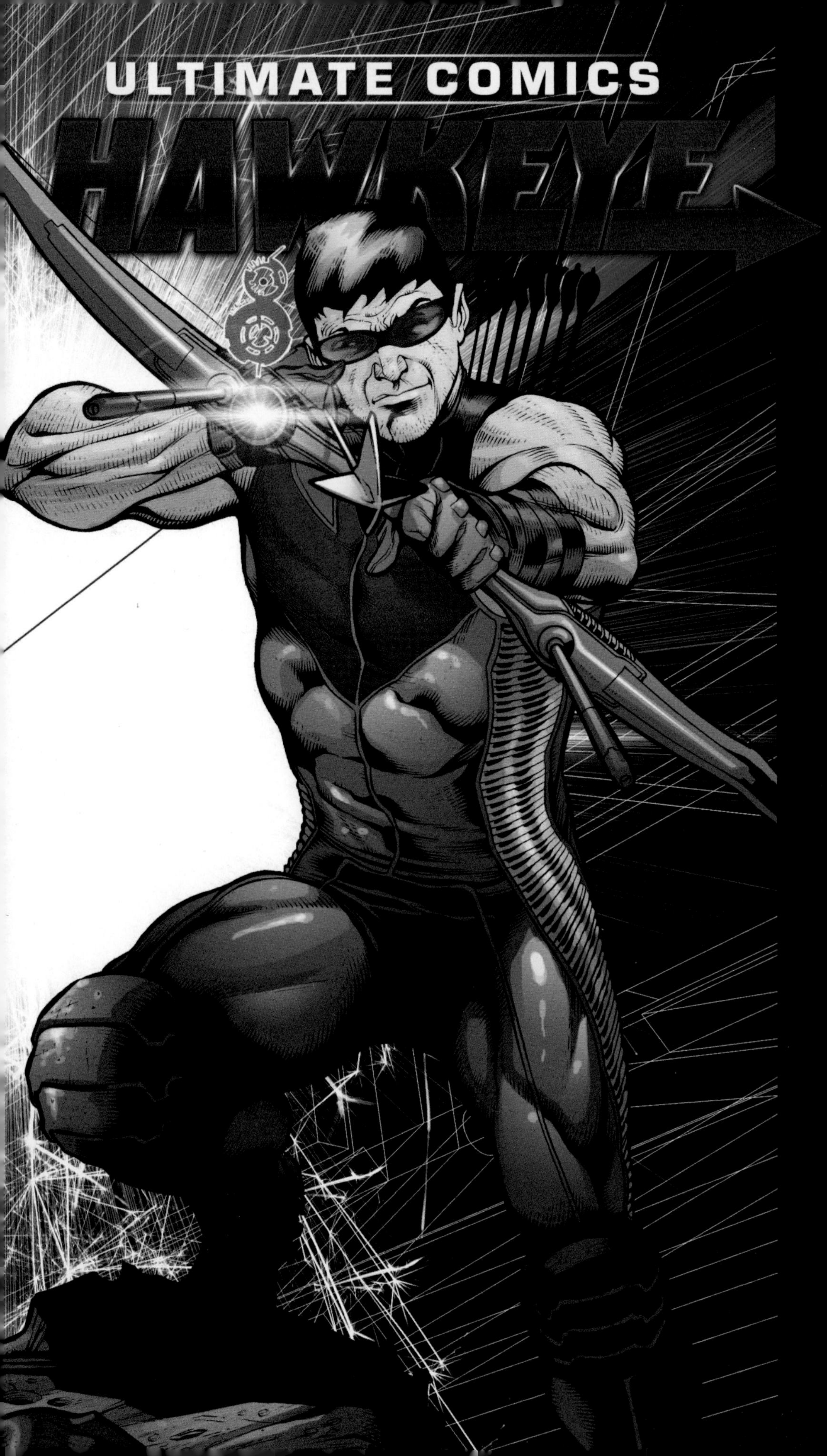
ULTIMATE COMICS
HAWKEYE

WRITER: **JONATHAN HICKMAN**

PENCILER: **RAFA SANDOVAL**

INKER: **JORDI TARRAGONA**

COLORIST: **BRAD ANDERSON**

LETTERER: **VC'S CLAYTON COWLES**

COVER ART: **KAARE ANDREWS**

ASSISTANT EDITOR: **JON MOISAN**

ASSOCIATE EDITOR: **SANA AMANAT**

SENIOR EDITOR: **MARK PANICCIA**

SPECIAL THANKS TO **CHRIS ELIOPOULOS** & **JOE SABINO**

COLLECTION EDITOR: **JENNIFER GRÜNWALD**

ASSISTANT EDITORS: **ALEX STARBUCK** & **NELSON RIBEIRO**

EDITOR, SPECIAL PROJECTS: **MARK D. BEAZLEY**

SENIOR EDITOR, SPECIAL PROJECTS: **JEFF YOUNGQUIST**

SENIOR VICE PRESIDENT OF SALES: **DAVID GABRIEL**

SVP OF BRAND PLANNING & COMMUNICATIONS: **MICHAEL PASCIULLO**

BOOK DESIGNER: **RODOLFO MURAGUCHI**

EDITOR IN CHIEF: **AXEL ALONSO**

CHIEF CREATIVE OFFICER: **JOE QUESADA**

PUBLISHER: **DAN BUCKLEY**

EXECUTIVE PRODUCER: **ALAN FINE**

Southwest Branch

1·0·2012

9010 36th Ave SW
Seattle, WA 98126-3821

ULTIMATE COMICS HAWKEYE BY JONATHAN HICKMAN. Contains material originally published in magazine form as ULTIMATE COMICS HAWKEYE #1-4. First printing 2011. Hardcover ISBN# 978-0-7851-6227-8. Softcover ISBN# 978-0-7851-5744-1. Published by MARVEL WORLDWIDE, INC., a subsidiary of MARVEL ENTERTAINMENT, LLC. OFFICE OF PUBLICATION: 135 West 50th Street, New York, NY 10020. Copyright © 2011 and 2012 Marvel Characters, Inc. All rights reserved. Hardcover: $19.99 per copy in the U.S. and $21.99 in Canada (GST #R127032852). Softcover: $14.99 per copy in the U.S. and $16.99 in Canada (GST #R127032852). Canadian Agreement #40668537. All characters featured in this issue and the distinctive names and likenesses thereof, and all related indicia are trademarks of Marvel Characters, Inc. No similarity between any of the names, characters, persons, and/or institutions in this magazine with those of any living or dead person or institution is intended, and any such similarity which may exist is purely coincidental. Printed in the U.S.A. ALAN FINE, EVP - Office of the President, Marvel Worldwide, Inc. and EVP & CMO Marvel Characters B.V.; DAN BUCKLEY, Publisher & President - Print, Animation & Digital Divisions; JOE QUESADA, Chief Creative Officer; DAVID BOGART, SVP of Business Affairs & Talent Management; TOM BREVOORT, SVP of Publishing; C.B. CEBULSKI, SVP of Creator & Content Development; DAVID GABRIEL, SVP of Publishing Sales & Circulation; MICHAEL PASCIULLO, SVP of Brand Planning & Communications; JIM O'KEEFE, VP of Operations & Logistics; DAN CARR, Executive Director of Publishing Technology; SUSAN CRESPI, Editorial Operations Manager; ALEX MORALES, Publishing Operations Manager; STAN LEE, Chairman Emeritus. For information regarding advertising in Marvel Comics or on Marvel.com, please contact John Dokes, VP Integrated Sales and Marketing, at jdokes@marvel.com. For Marvel subscription inquiries, please call 800-217-9158. **Manufactured between 11/28/2011 and 1/2/2012 (hardcover), and 11/28/2011 and 1/9/2012 (softcover), by R.R. DONNELLEY, INC., SALEM, VA, USA.**

10 9 8 7 6 5 4 3 2 1

1

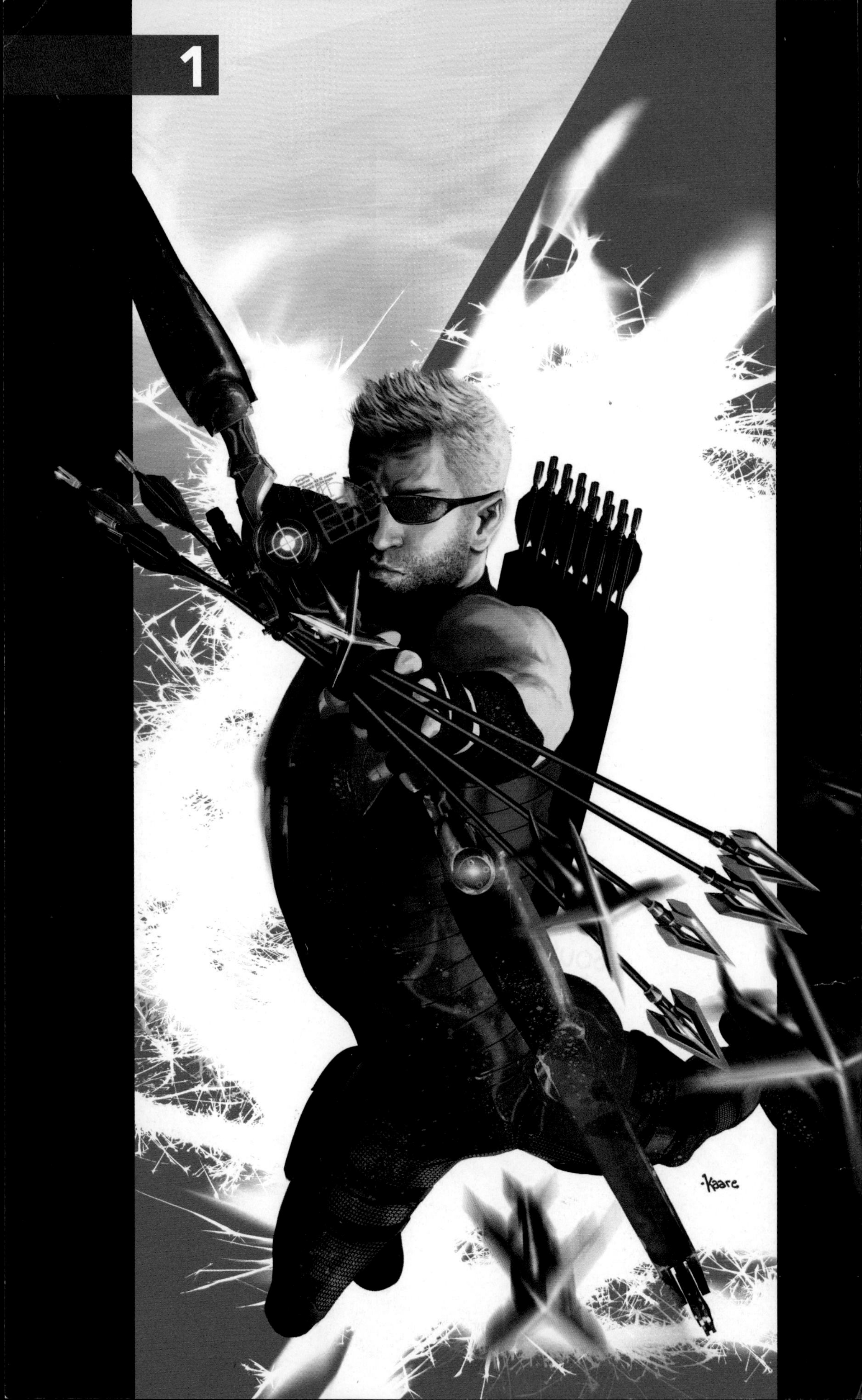
Kaare

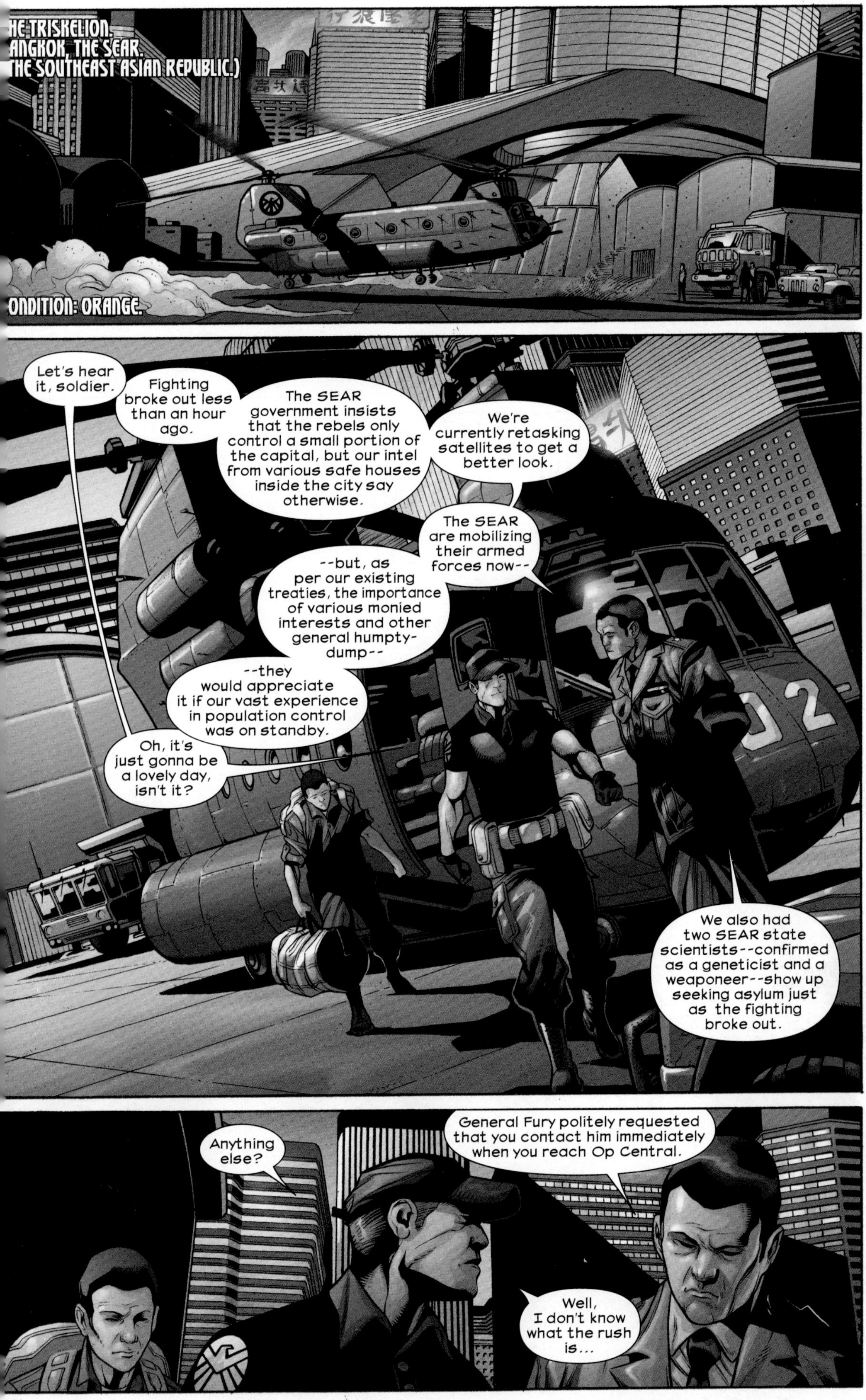

HE TRISKELION.
ANGKOK, THE SEAR.
THE SOUTHEAST ASIAN REPUBLIC.)
ONDITION: ORANGE.
Let's hear it, soldier.
Fighting broke out less than an hour ago.
The SEAR government insists that the rebels only control a small portion of the capital, but our intel from various safe houses inside the city say otherwise.
We're currently retasking satellites to get a better look.
The SEAR are mobilizing their armed forces now--
--but, as per our existing treaties, the importance of various monied interests and other general humpty-dump--
--they would appreciate it if our vast experience in population control was on standby.
Oh, it's just gonna be a lovely day, isn't it?
We also had two SEAR state scientists--confirmed as a geneticist and a weaponeer--show up seeking asylum just as the fighting broke out.
Anything else?
General Fury politely requested that you contact him immediately when you reach Op Central.
Well, I don't know what the rush is...

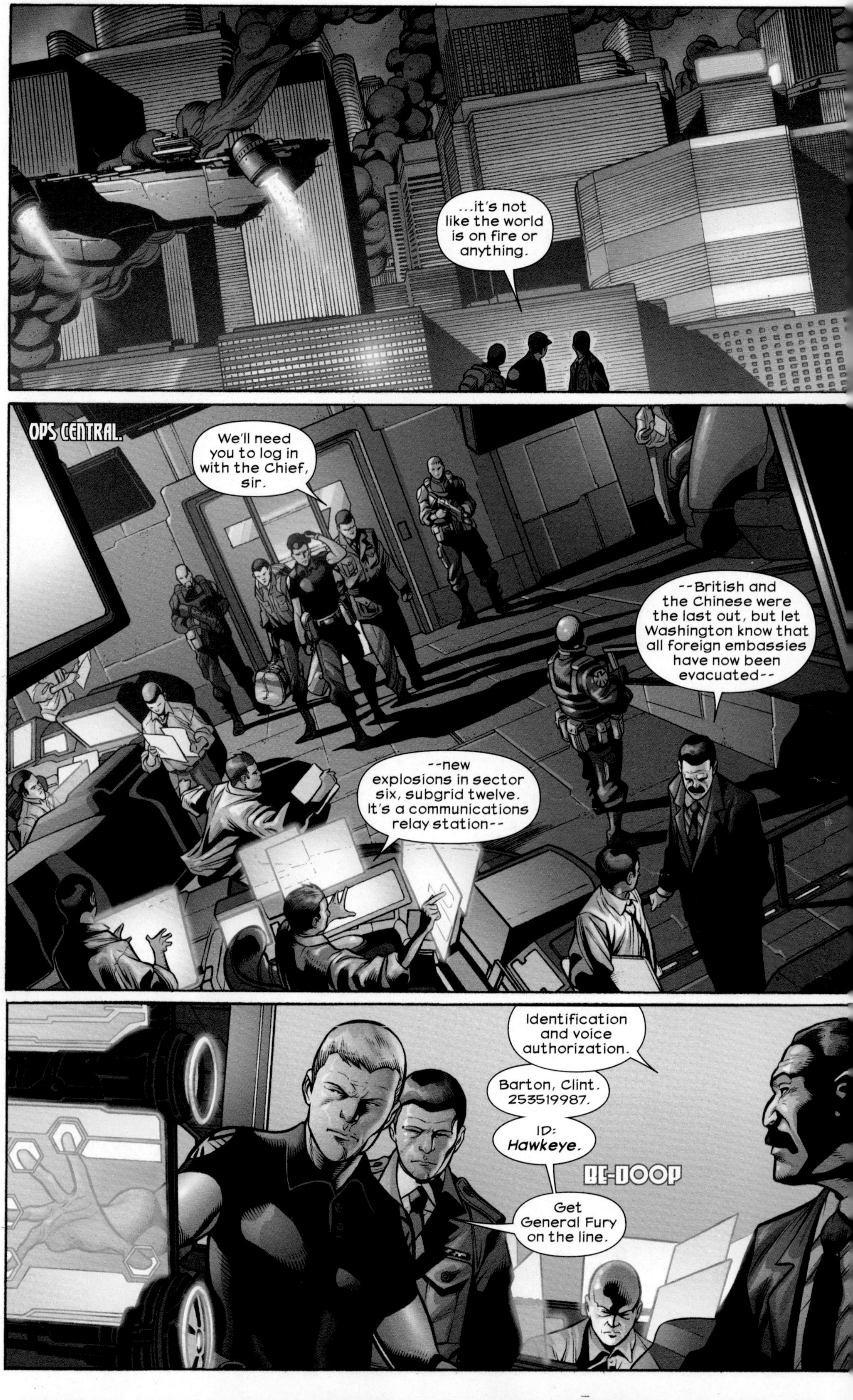
...it's not like the world is on fire or anything.
OPS CENTRAL.
We'll need you to log in with the Chief, sir.
--British and the Chinese were the last out, but let Washington know that all foreign embassies have now been evacuated--
--new explosions in sector six, subgrid twelve. It's a communications relay station--
Identification and voice authorization.
Barton, Clint. 253519987.
ID: *Hawkeye.*
BE-DOOP
Get General Fury on the line.

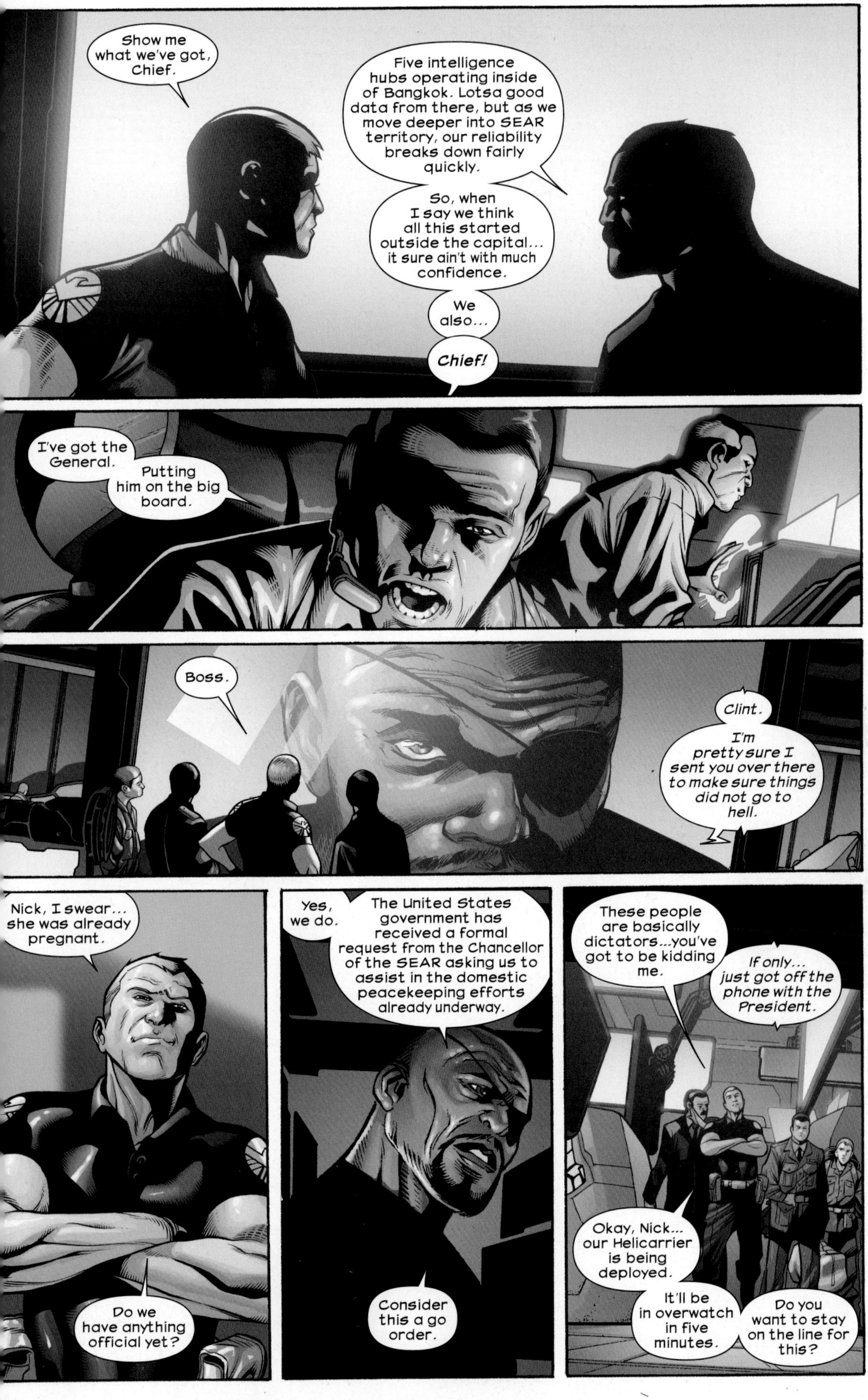
Show me what we've got, Chief.
Five intelligence hubs operating inside of Bangkok. Lotsa good data from there, but as we move deeper into SEAR territory, our reliability breaks down fairly quickly.
So, when I say we think all this started outside the capital... it sure ain't with much confidence.
We also...
Chief!
I've got the General.
Putting him on the big board.
Boss.
Clint.
I'm pretty sure I sent you over there to make sure things did not go to hell.
Nick, I swear... she was already pregnant.
Do we have anything official yet?
Yes, we do.
The United States government has received a formal request from the Chancellor of the SEAR asking us to assist in the domestic peacekeeping efforts already underway.
Consider this a go order.
These people are basically dictators...you've got to be kidding me.
If only... just got off the phone with the President.
Okay, Nick... our Helicarrier is being deployed.
It'll be in overwatch in five minutes.
Do you want to stay on the line for this?

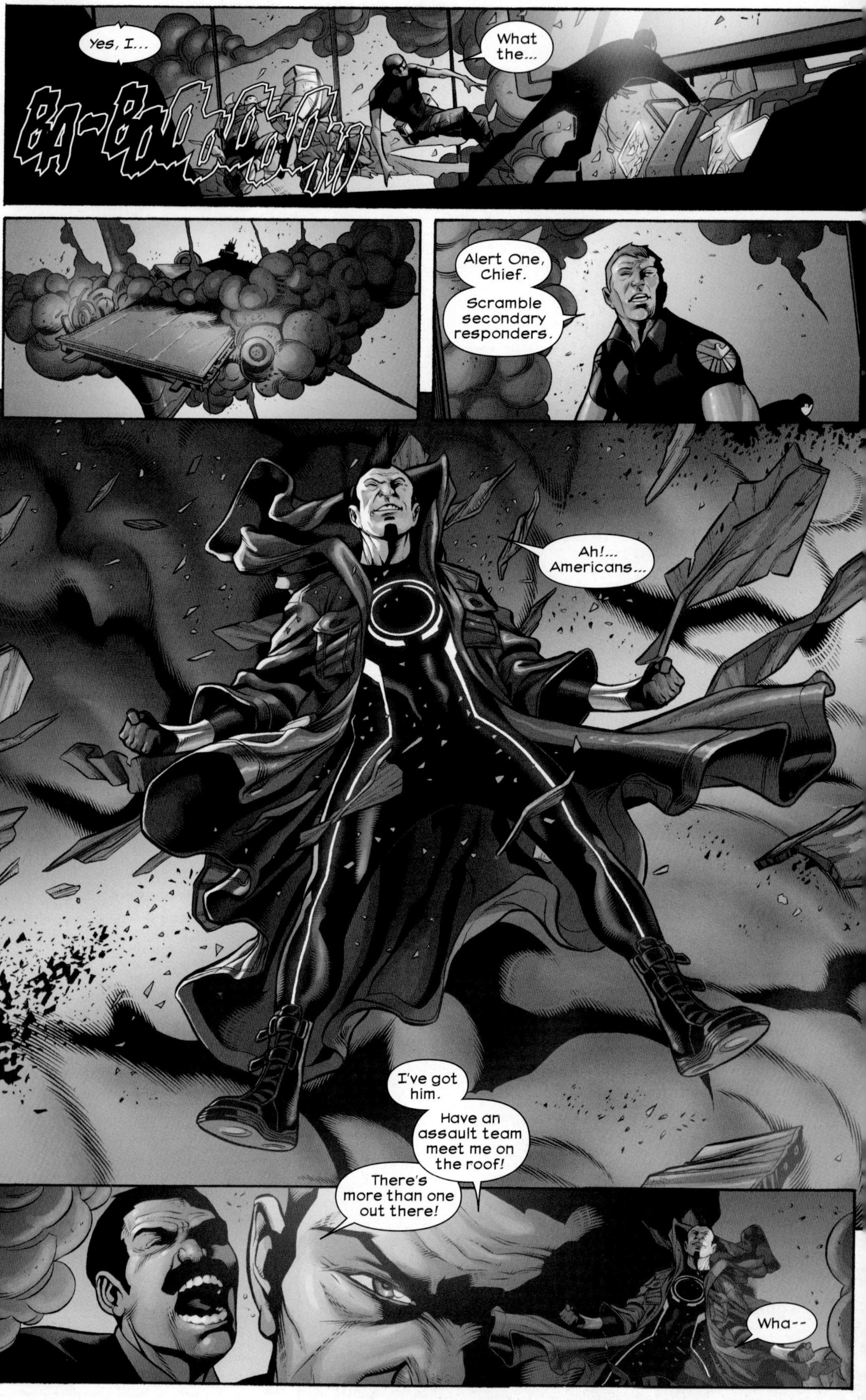
Yes, I...
BA-BOOOOOOOM
What the...
Alert One, Chief.
Scramble secondary responders.
Ah!... Americans...
I've got him.
Have an assault team meet me on the roof!
There's more than one out there!
Wha--

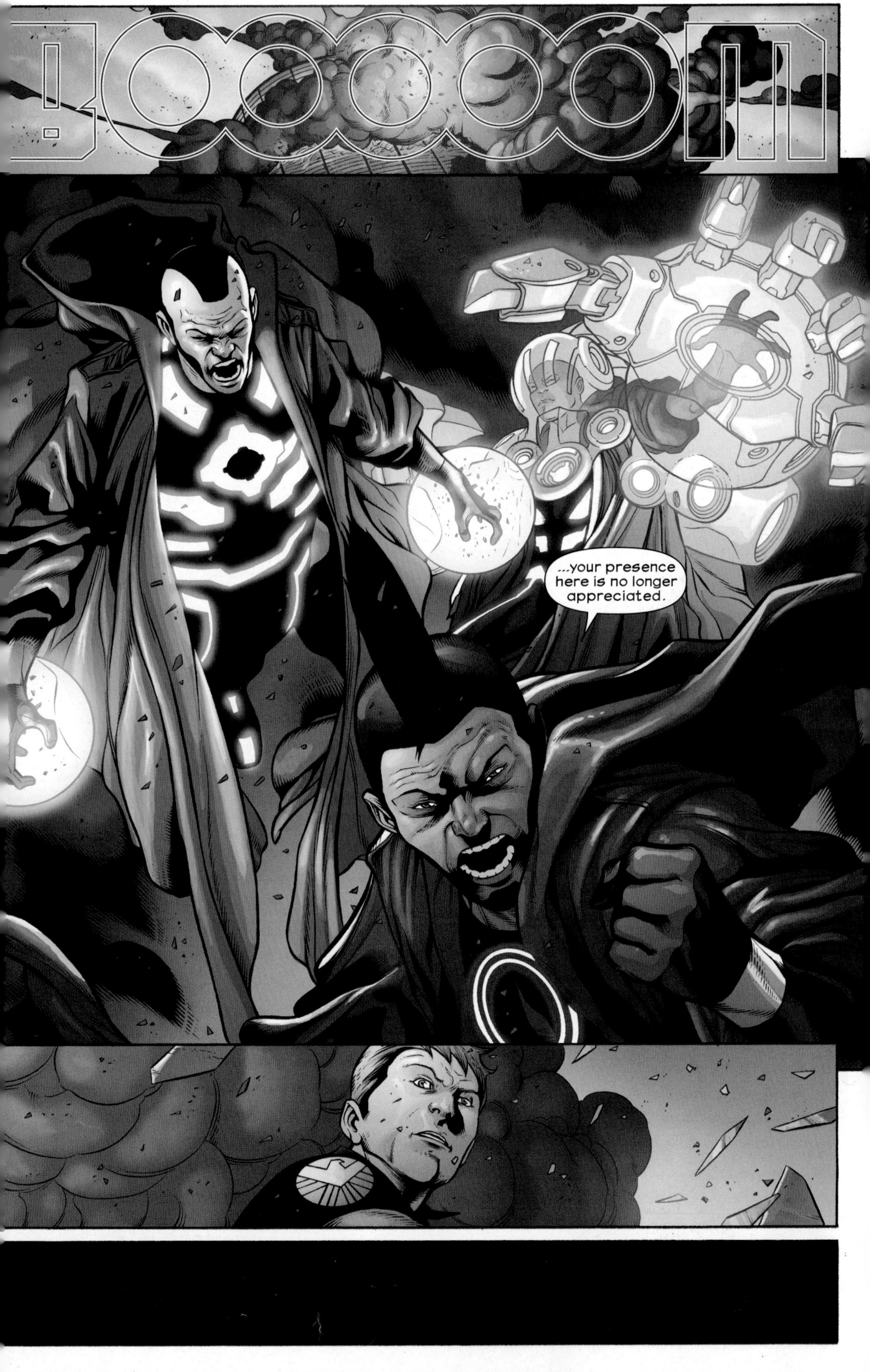
...your presence here is no longer appreciated.

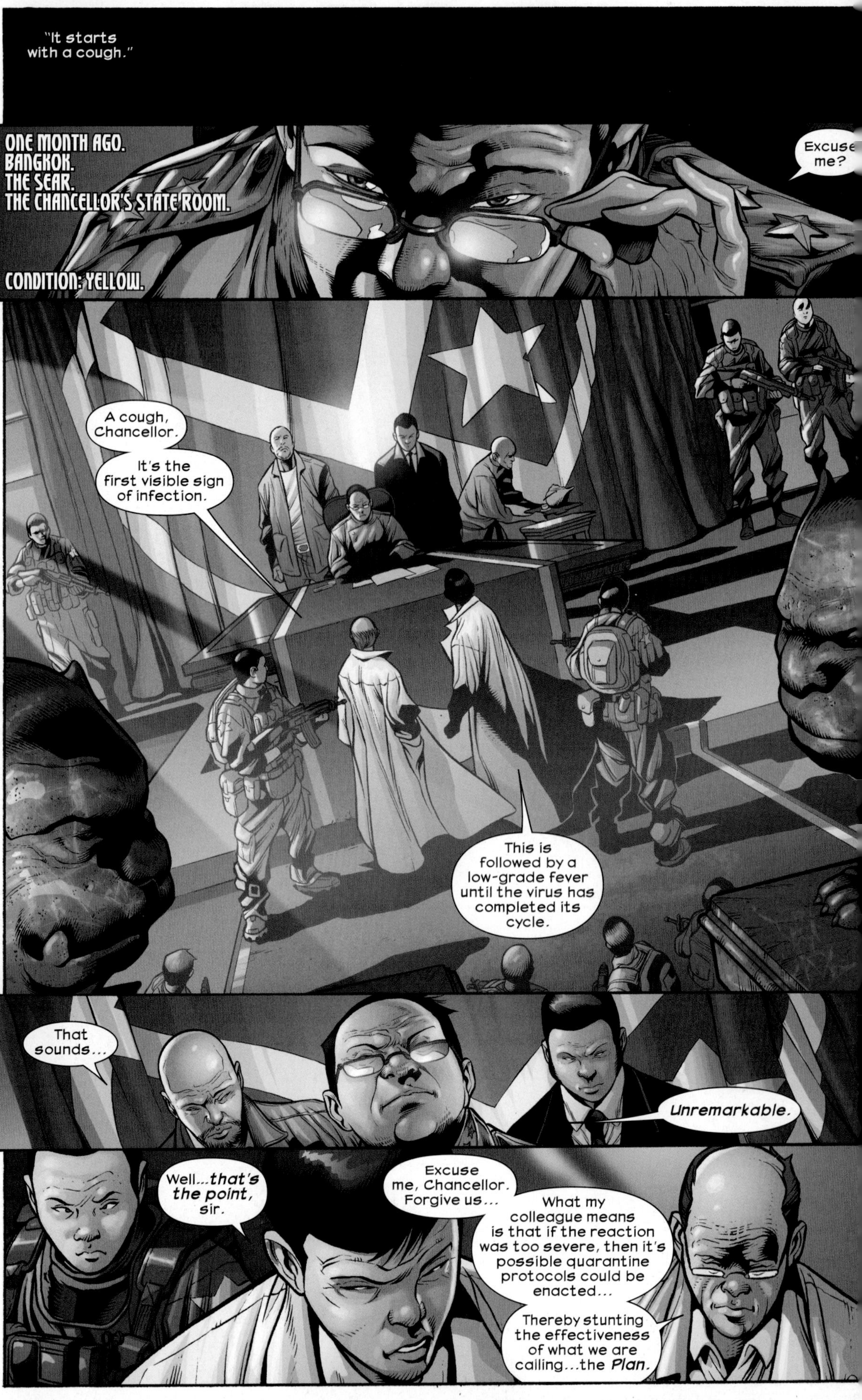
"It starts with a cough."
ONE MONTH AGO.
BANGKOK.
THE SEAR.
THE CHANCELLOR'S STATE ROOM.
CONDITION: YELLOW.
Excuse me?
A cough, Chancellor.
It's the first visible sign of infection.
This is followed by a low-grade fever until the virus has completed its cycle.
That sounds...
Unremarkable.
Well...*that's the point,* sir.
Excuse me, Chancellor. Forgive us...
What my colleague means is that if the reaction was too severe, then it's possible quarantine protocols could be enacted...
Thereby stunting the effectiveness of what we are calling...the *Plan.*

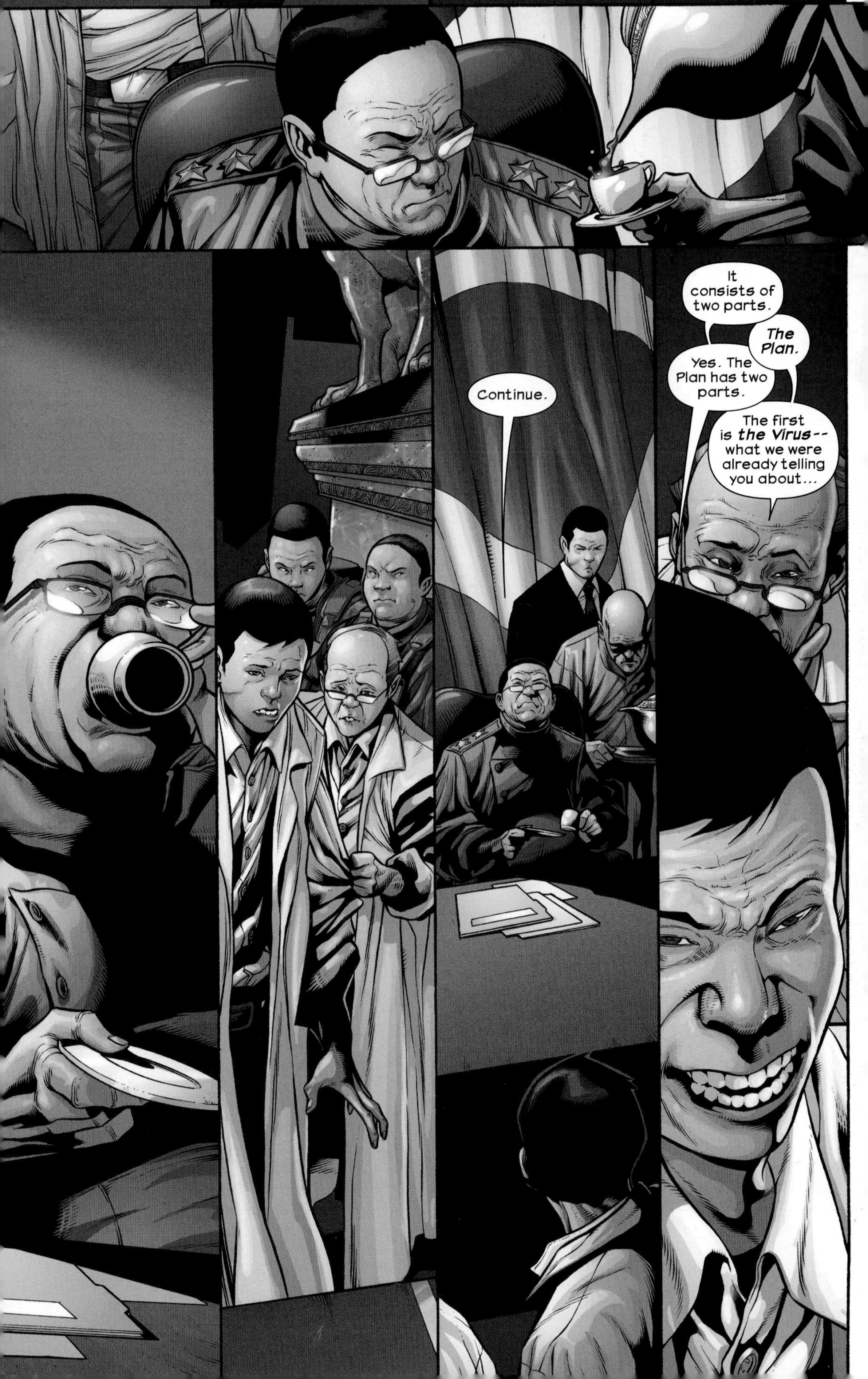

Continue.
It consists of two parts.
The Plan.
Yes. The Plan has two parts.
The first is the Virus--what we were already telling you about...

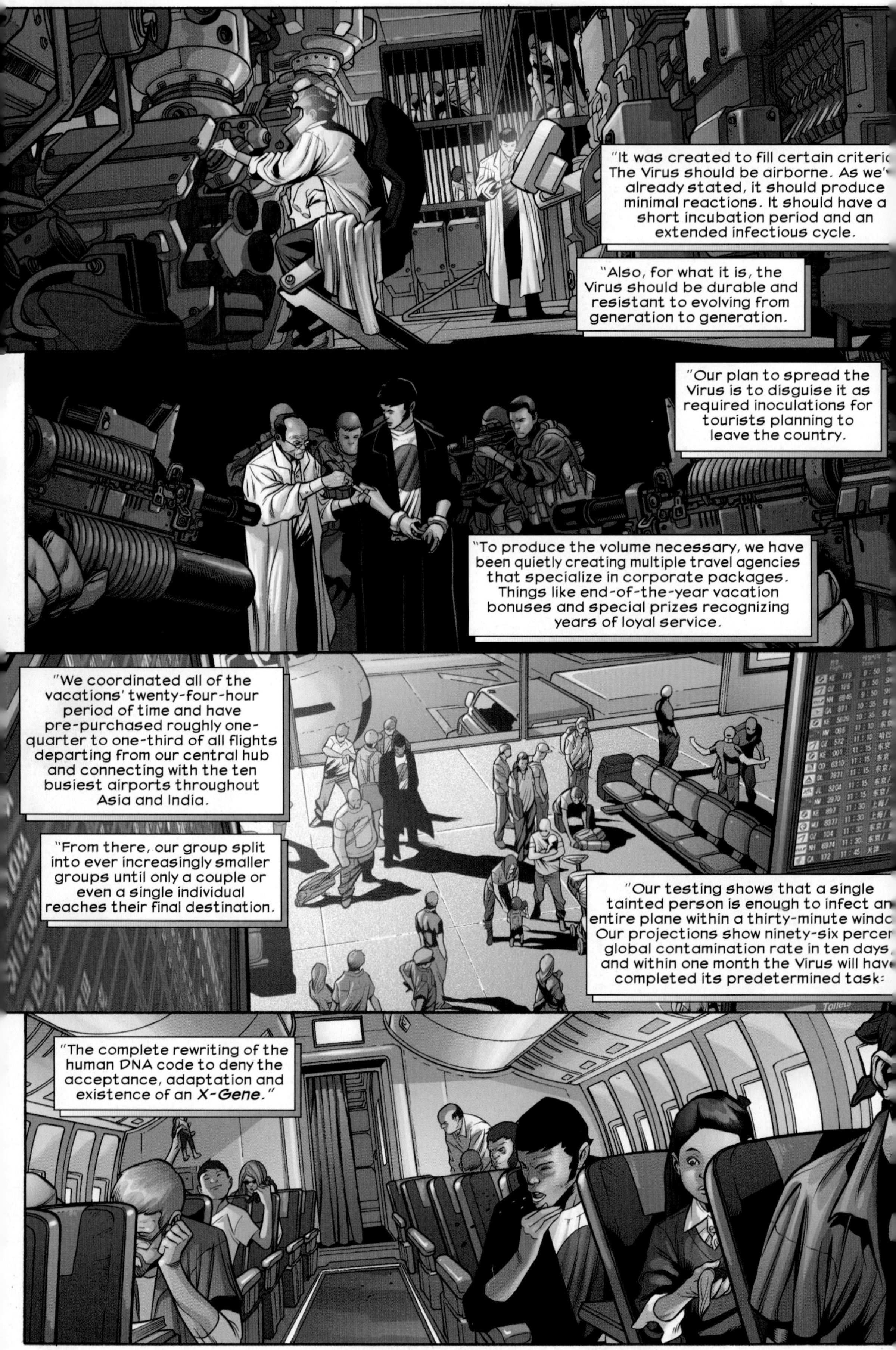
"It was created to fill certain criteri The Virus should be airborne. As we' already stated, it should produce minimal reactions. It should have a short incubation period and an extended infectious cycle.
"Also, for what it is, the Virus should be durable and resistant to evolving from generation to generation.
"Our plan to spread the Virus is to disguise it as required inoculations for tourists planning to leave the country.
"To produce the volume necessary, we have been quietly creating multiple travel agencies that specialize in corporate packages. Things like end-of-the-year vacation bonuses and special prizes recognizing years of loyal service.
"We coordinated all of the vacations' twenty-four-hour period of time and have pre-purchased roughly one-quarter to one-third of all flights departing from our central hub and connecting with the ten busiest airports throughout Asia and India.
"From there, our group split into ever increasingly smaller groups until only a couple or even a single individual reaches their final destination.
"Our testing shows that a single tainted person is enough to infect an entire plane within a thirty-minute windo Our projections show ninety-six percer global contamination rate in ten days, and within one month the Virus will hav completed its predetermined task:
Toilets
"The complete rewriting of the human DNA code to deny the acceptance, adaptation and existence of an *X-Gene.*"

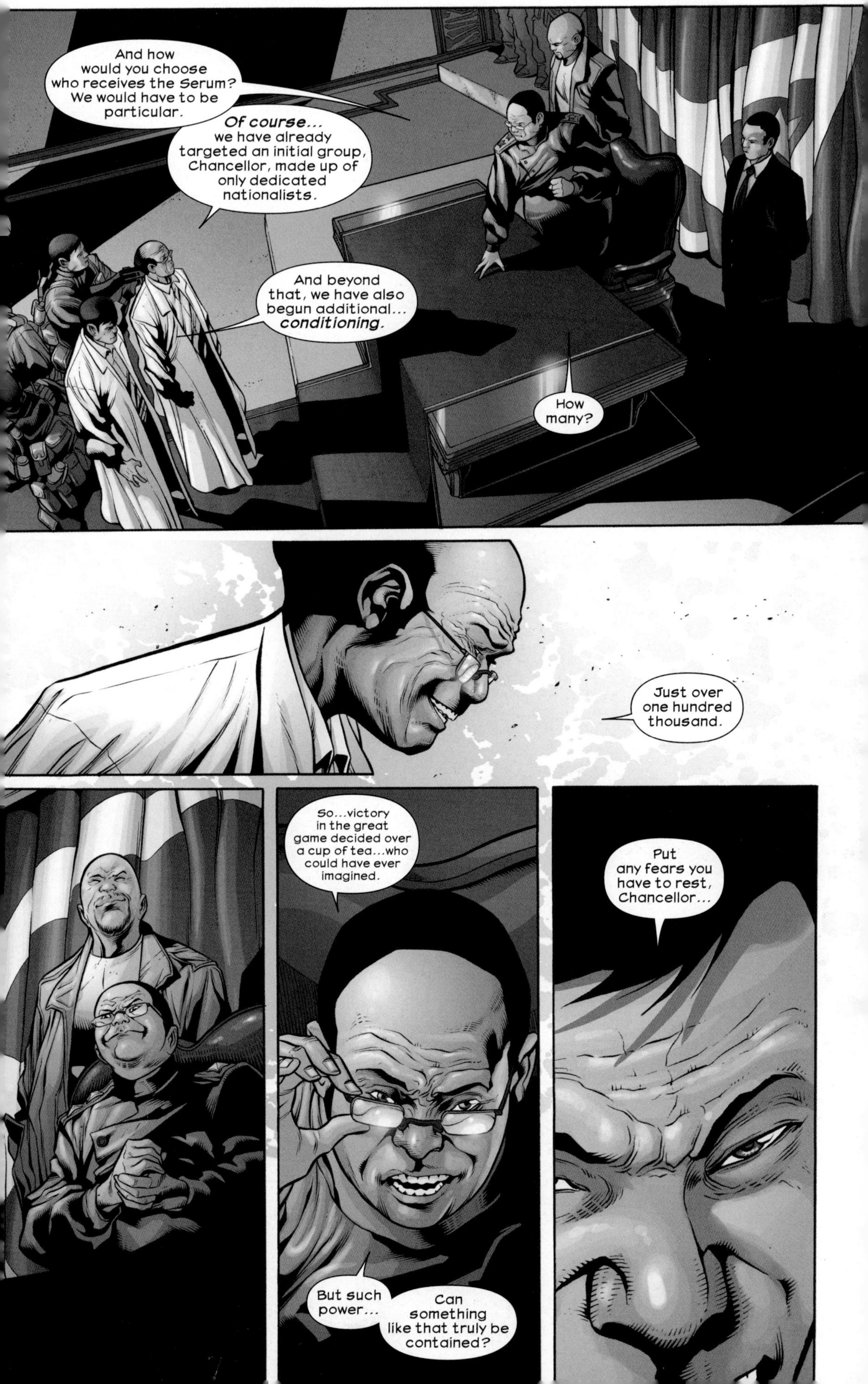
And how would you choose who receives the Serum? We would have to be particular.
Of course... we have already targeted an initial group, Chancellor, made up of only dedicated nationalists.
And beyond that, we have also begun additional... conditioning.
How many?
Just over one hundred thousand.
So...victory in the great game decided over a cup of tea...who could have ever imagined.
But such power...
Can something like that truly be contained?
Put any fears you have to rest, Chancellor...

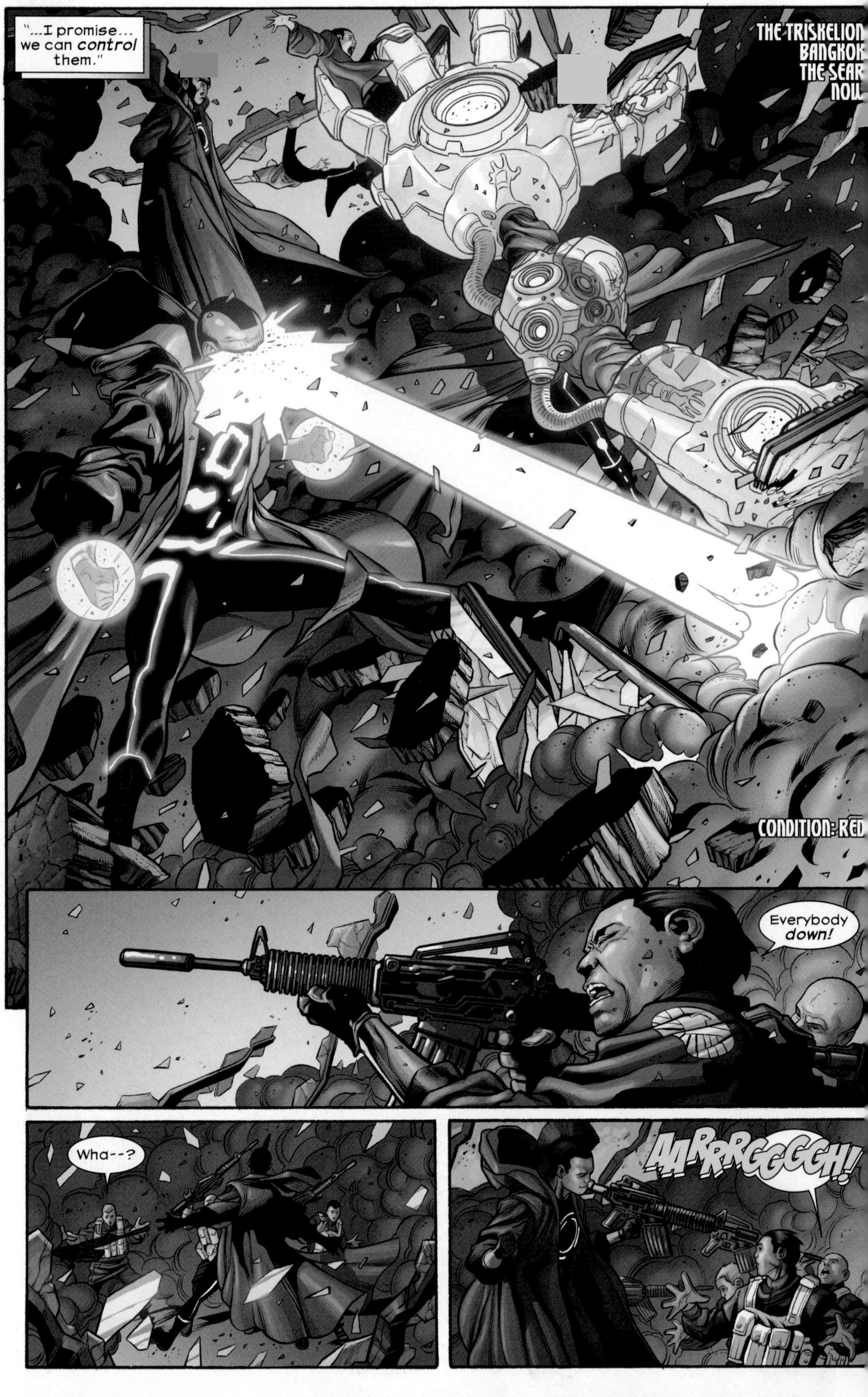
"...I promise... we can control them."
THE TRISKELION BANGKOK THE SEAR NOW
CONDITION: RED
Everybody down!
Wha--?
AARRRGGGGH!

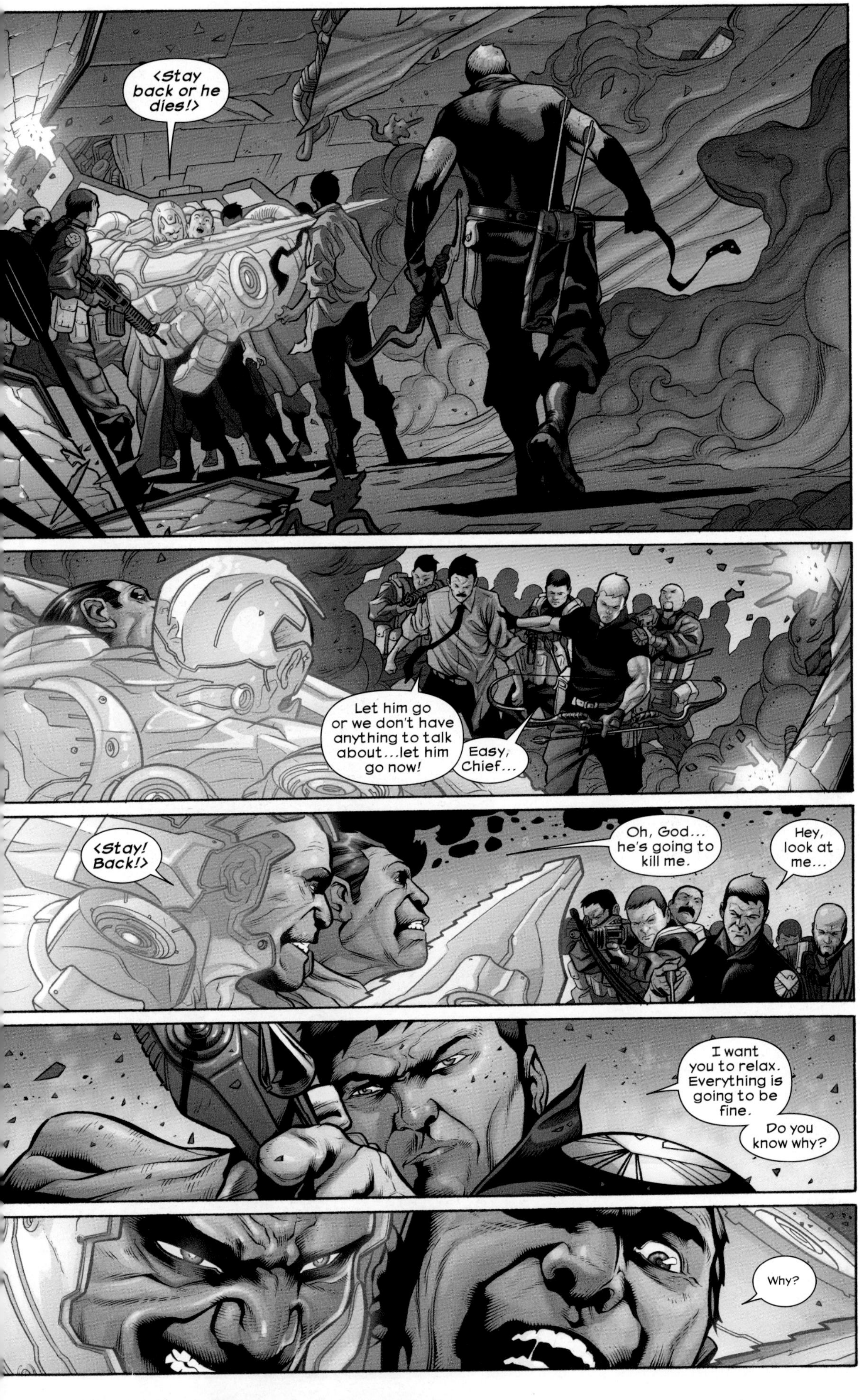
<Stay back or he dies!>
Let him go or we don't have anything to talk about...let him go now!
Easy, Chief...
<Stay! Back!>
Oh, God... he's going to kill me.
Hey, look at me...
I want you to relax. Everything is going to be fine.
Do you know why?
Why?

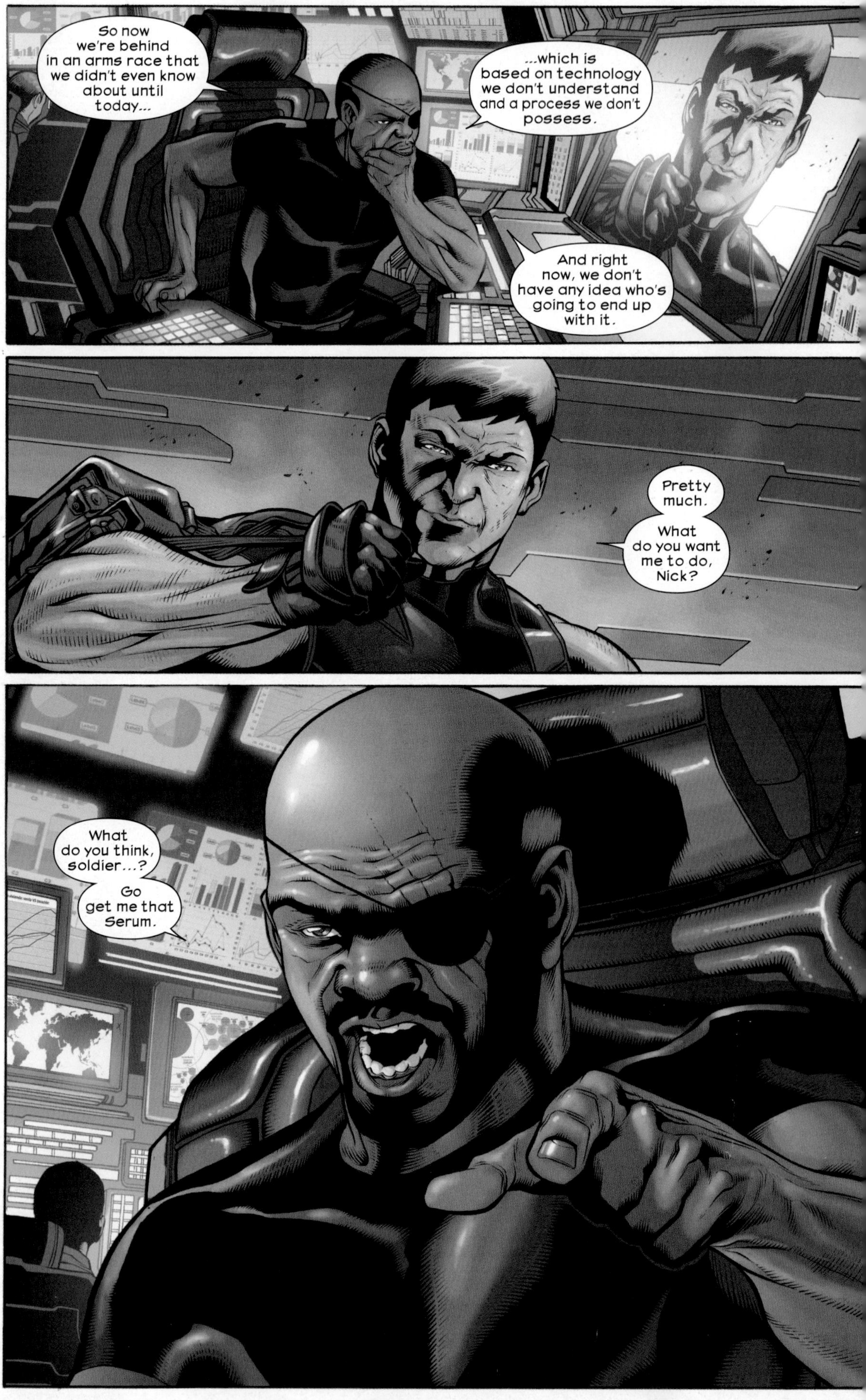
So now we're behind in an arms race that we didn't even know about until today...
...which is based on technology we don't understand and a process we don't possess.
And right now, we don't have any idea who's going to end up with it.
Pretty much.
What do you want me to do, Nick?
What do you think, soldier...?
Go get me that Serum.

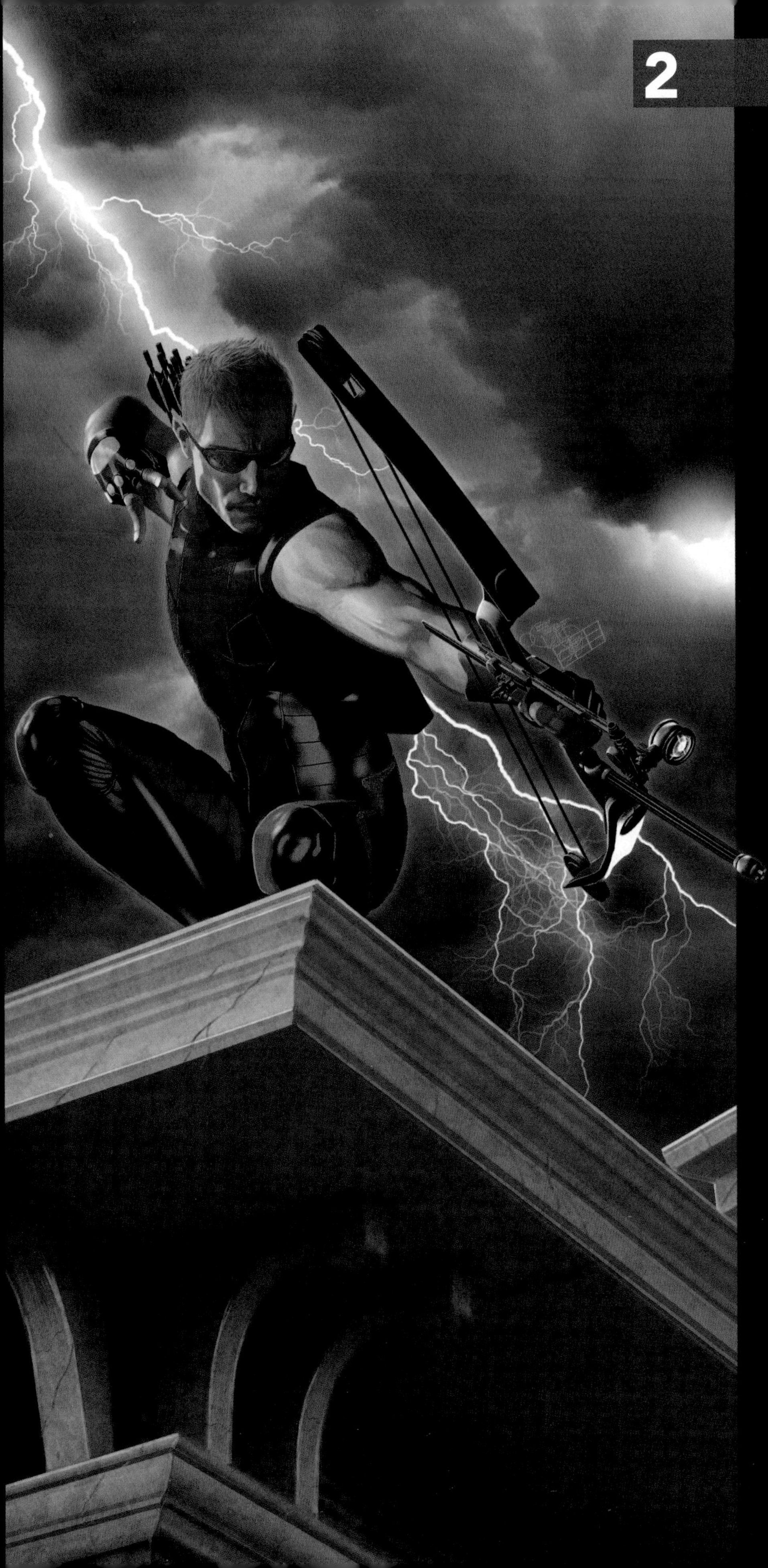

2

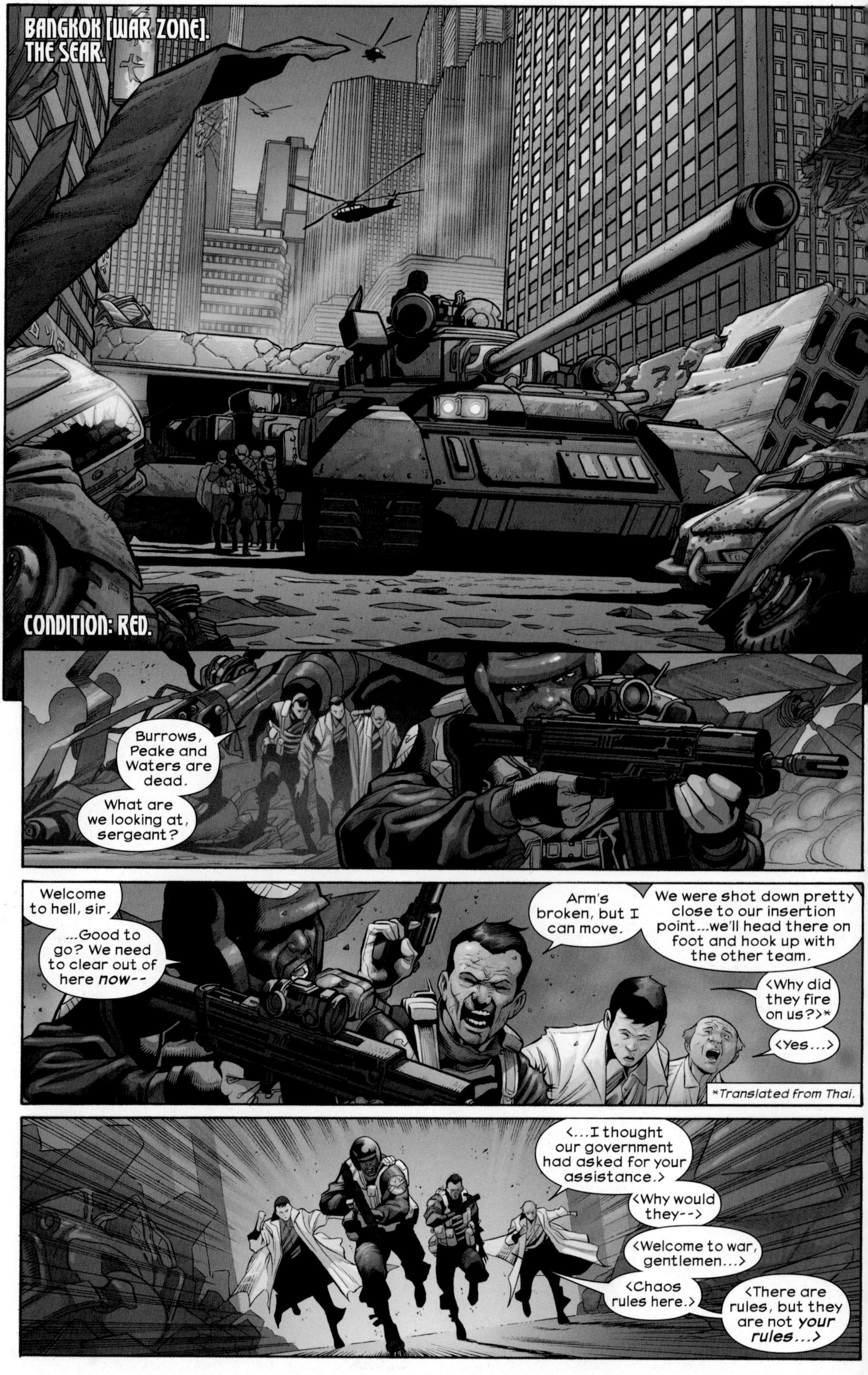
BANGKOK [WAR ZONE].
THE SEAR.
CONDITION: RED.
Burrows, Peake and Waters are dead.
What are we looking at, sergeant?
Welcome to hell, sir.
...Good to go? We need to clear out of here *now*--
Arm's broken, but I can move.
We were shot down pretty close to our insertion point...we'll head there on foot and hook up with the other team.
<Why did they fire on us?>*
<Yes...>
*Translated from Thai.
<...I thought our government had asked for your assistance.>
<Why would they-->
<Welcome to war, gentlemen...>
<Chaos rules here.>
<There are rules, but they are not *your rules*...>

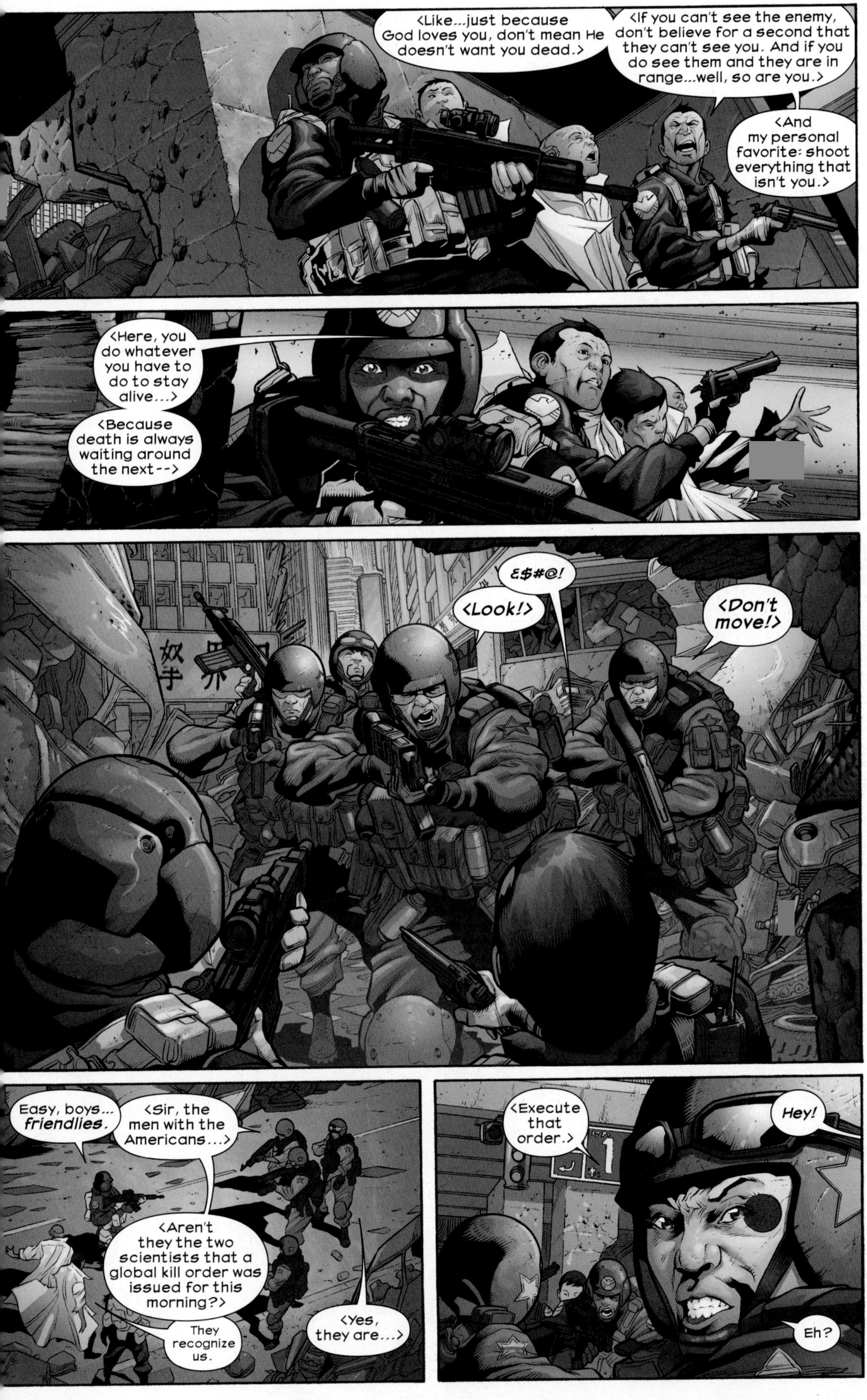

<Like...just because God loves you, don't mean He doesn't want you dead.>
<If you can't see the enemy, don't believe for a second that they can't see you. And if you do see them and they are in range...well, so are you.>
<And my personal favorite: shoot everything that isn't you.>
<Here, you do whatever you have to do to stay alive...>
<Because death is always waiting around the next-->
&$#@!
<Look!>
<Don't move!>
Easy, boys... *friendlies.*
<Sir, the men with the Americans...>
<Aren't they the two scientists that a global kill order was issued for this morning?>
They recognize us.
<Yes, they are...>
<Execute that order.>
Hey!
Eh?

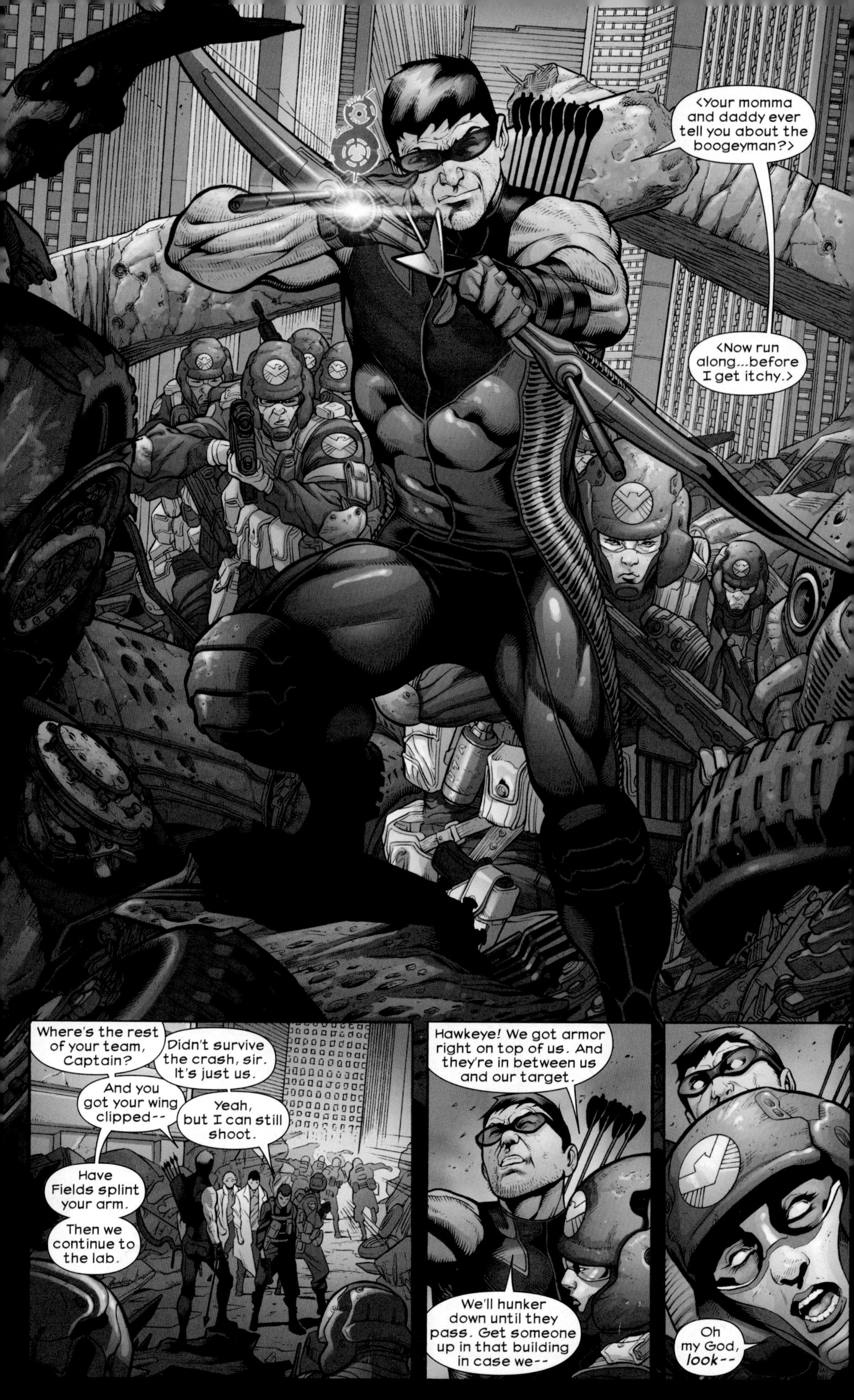
<Your momma and daddy ever tell you about the boogeyman?>
<Now run along...before I get itchy.>
Where's the rest of your team, Captain?
Didn't survive the crash, sir. It's just us.
And you got your wing clipped--
Yeah, but I can still shoot.
Have Fields splint your arm.
Then we continue to the lab.
Hawkeye! We got armor right on top of us. And they're in between us and our target.
We'll hunker down until they pass. Get someone up in that building in case we--
Oh my God, look--

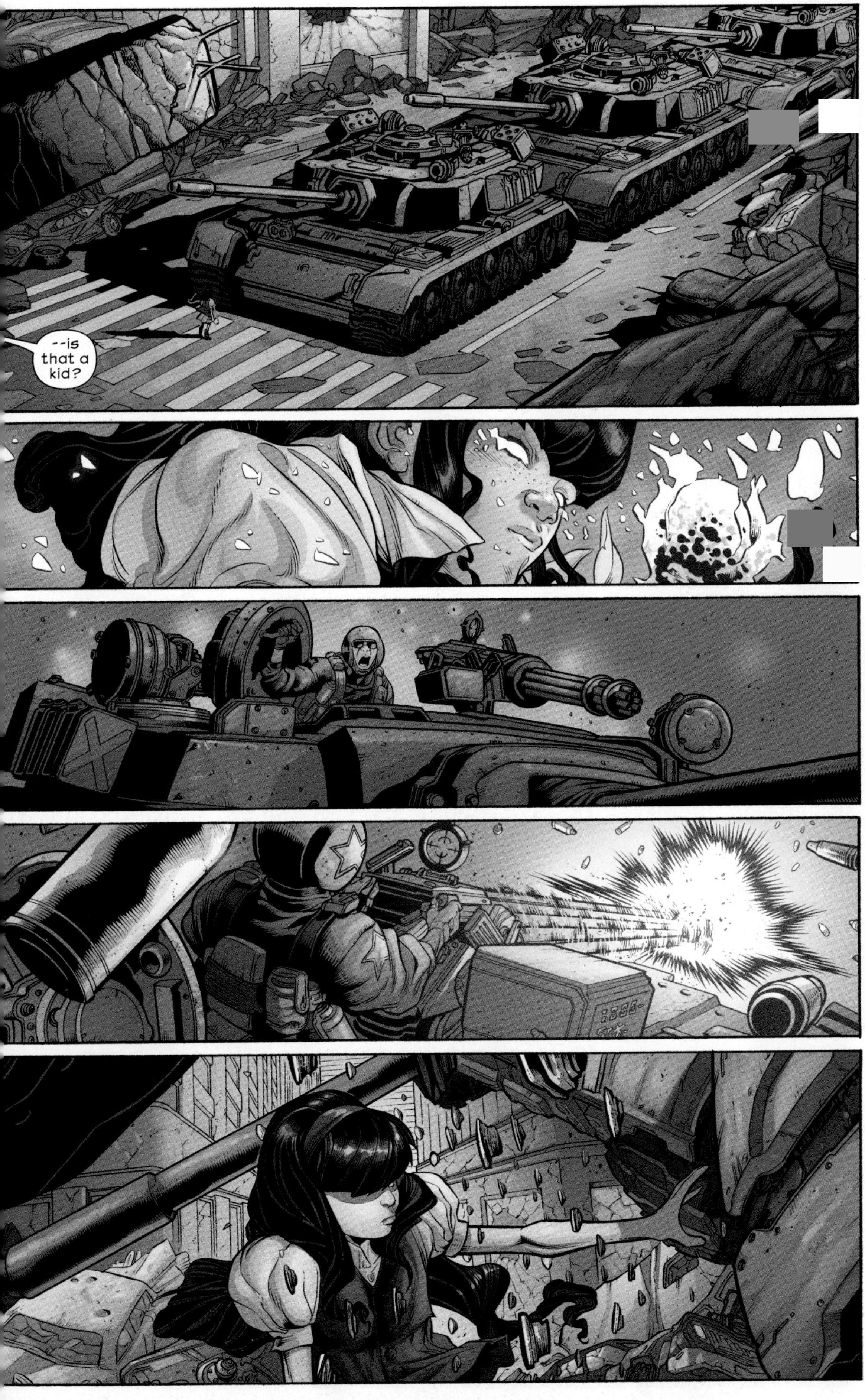
--is that a kid?

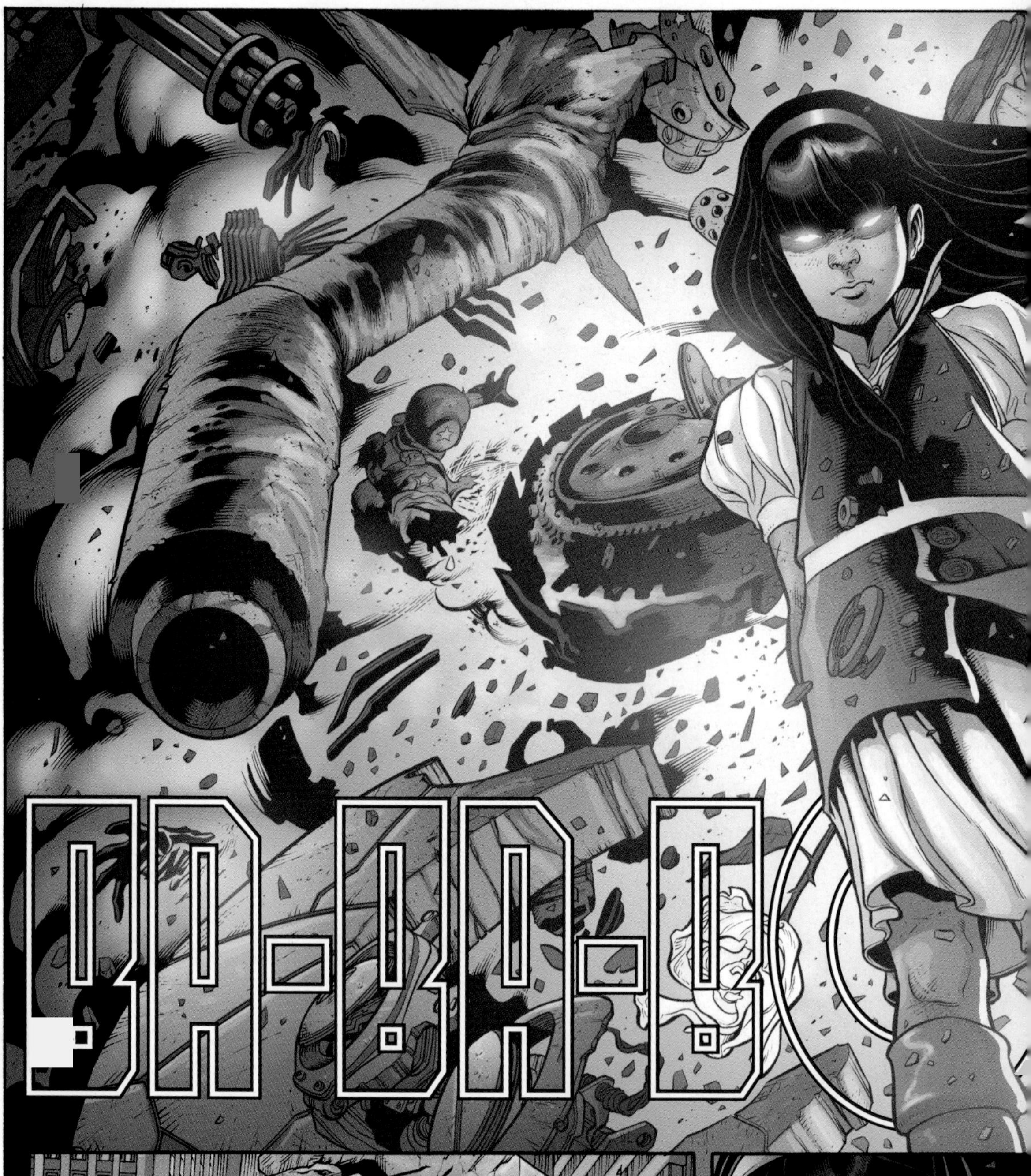

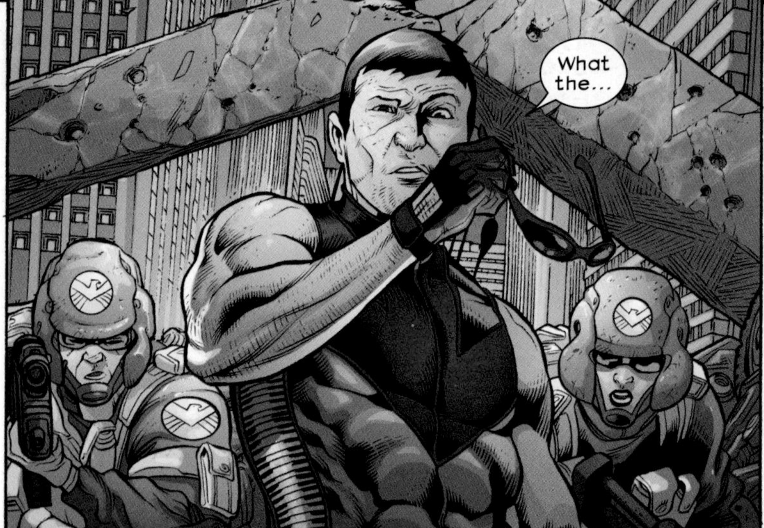
What the...

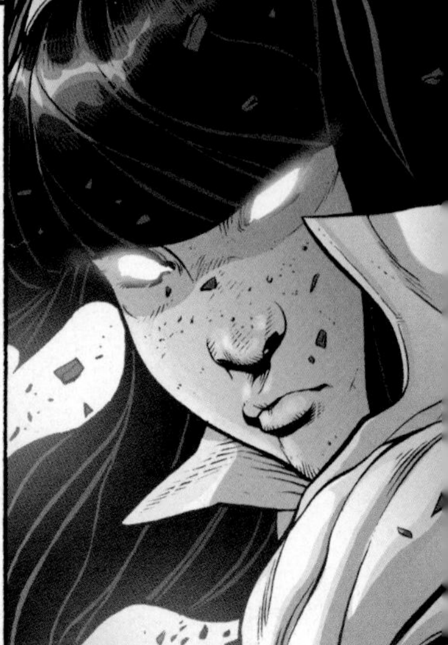

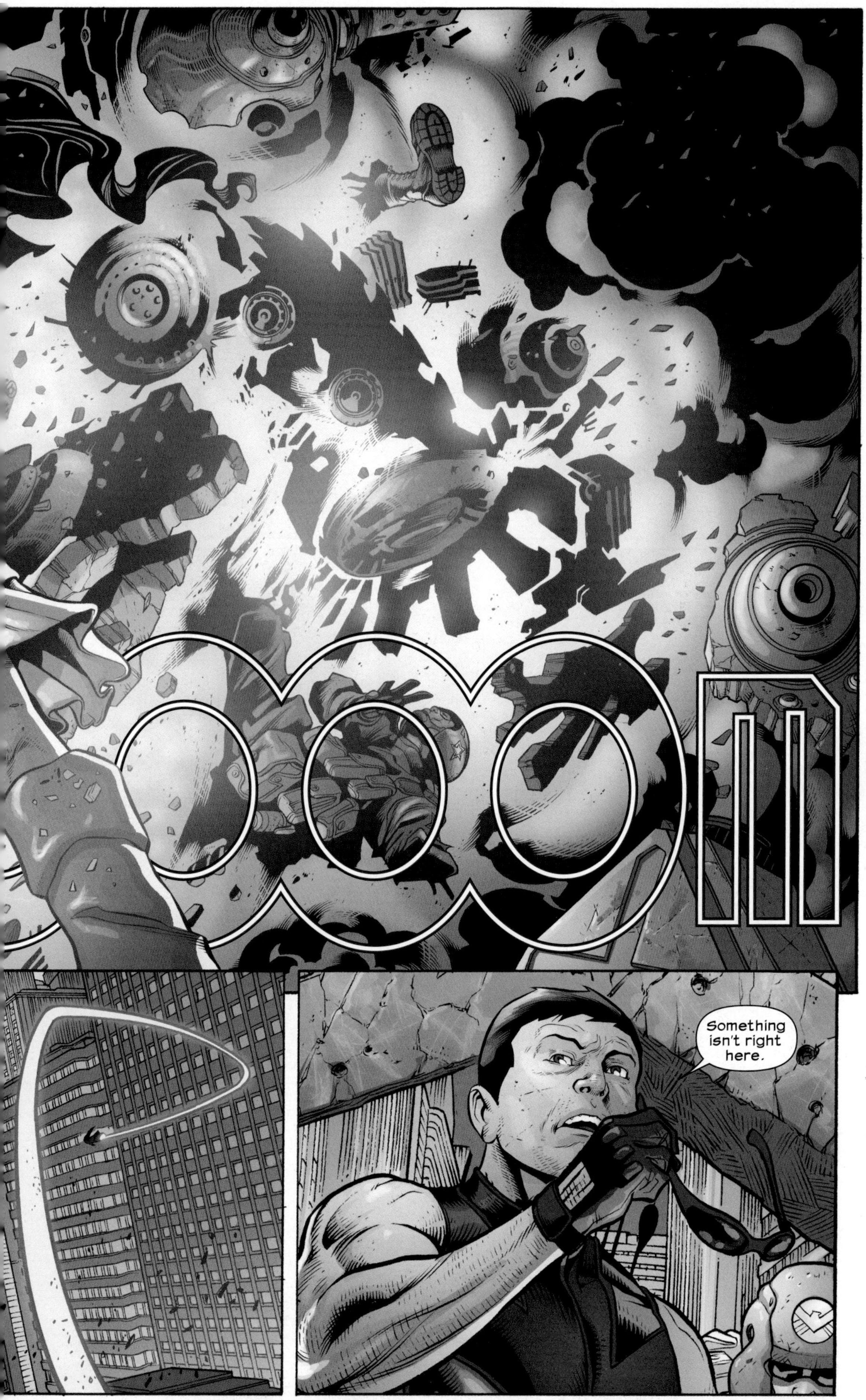
BOOOM
Something isn't right here.

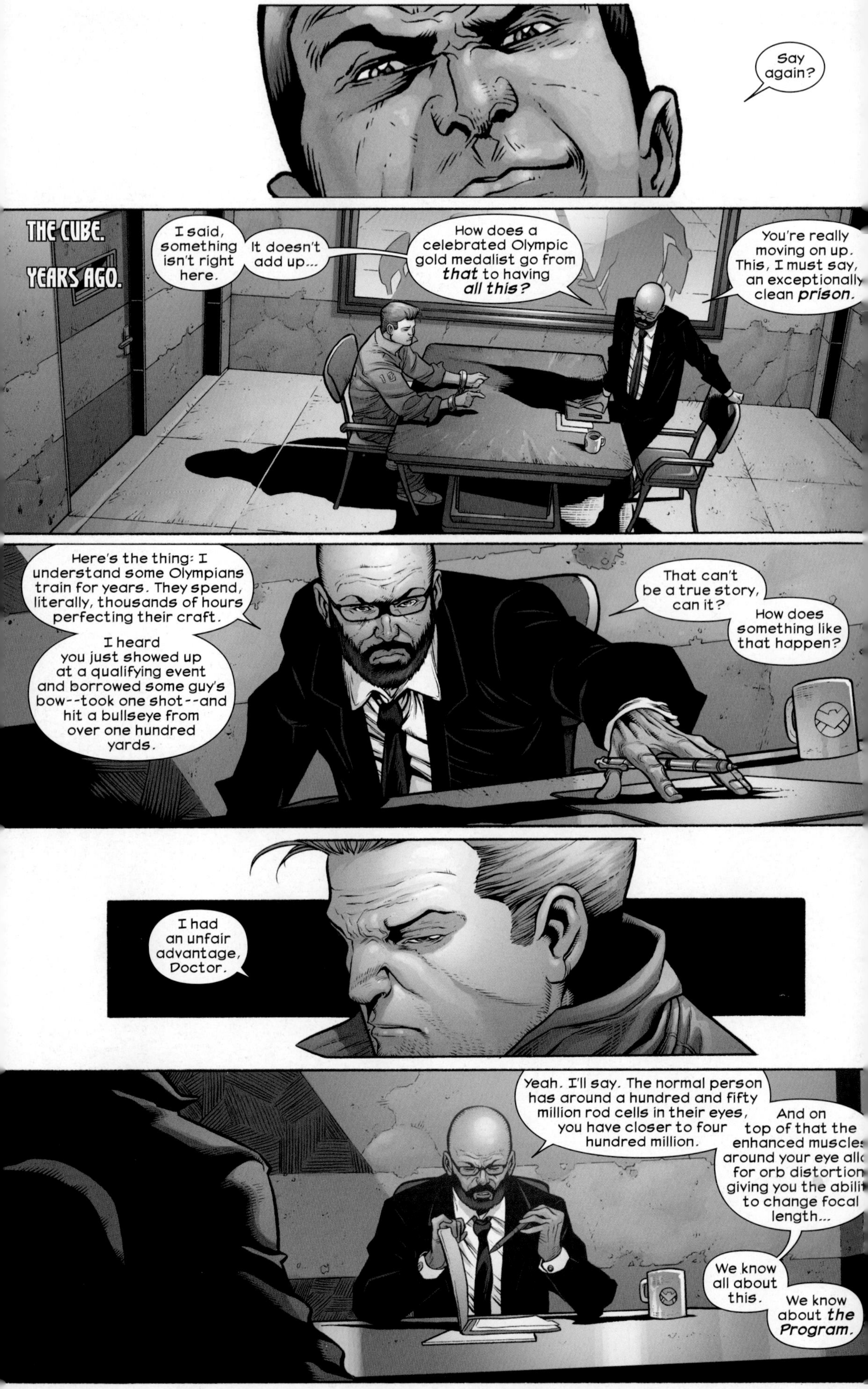
Say again?
THE CUBE.
YEARS AGO.
I said, something isn't right here.
It doesn't add up...
How does a celebrated Olympic gold medalist go from *that* to having *all this?*
You're really moving on up. This, I must say, an exceptionally clean *prison.*
Here's the thing: I understand some Olympians train for years. They spend, literally, thousands of hours perfecting their craft.
I heard you just showed up at a qualifying event and borrowed some guy's bow--took one shot--and hit a bullseye from over one hundred yards.
That can't be a true story, can it?
How does something like that happen?
I had an unfair advantage, Doctor.
Yeah. I'll say. The normal person has around a hundred and fifty million rod cells in their eyes, you have closer to four hundred million.
We know all about this.
We know about *the Program.*

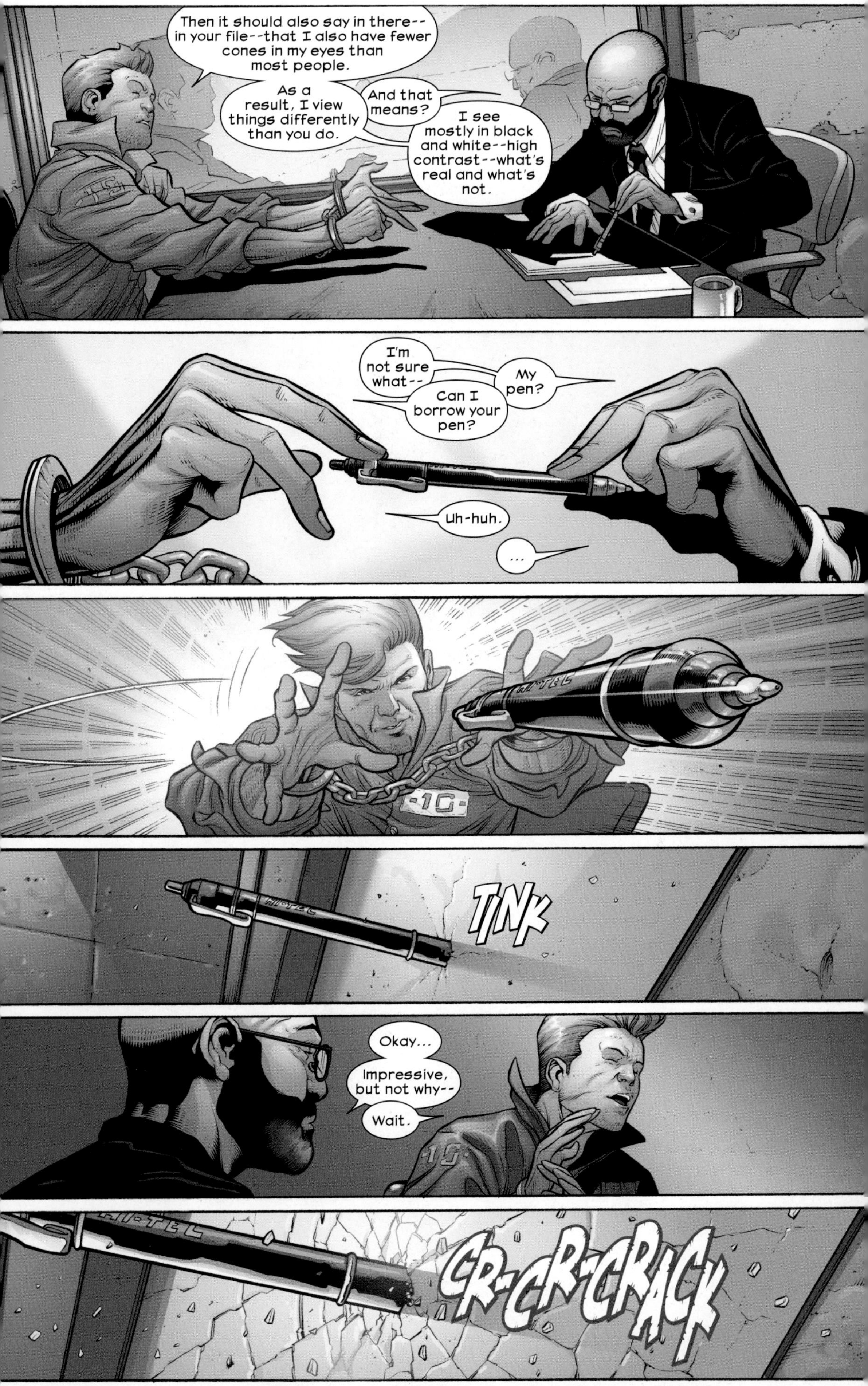
Then it should also say in there--in your file--that I also have fewer cones in my eyes than most people.
As a result, I view things differently than you do.
And that means?
I see mostly in black and white--high contrast--what's real and what's not.
I'm not sure what--
Can I borrow your pen?
My pen?
Uh-huh.
...
TINK
Okay...
Impressive, but not why--
Wait.
CR-CR-CRACK

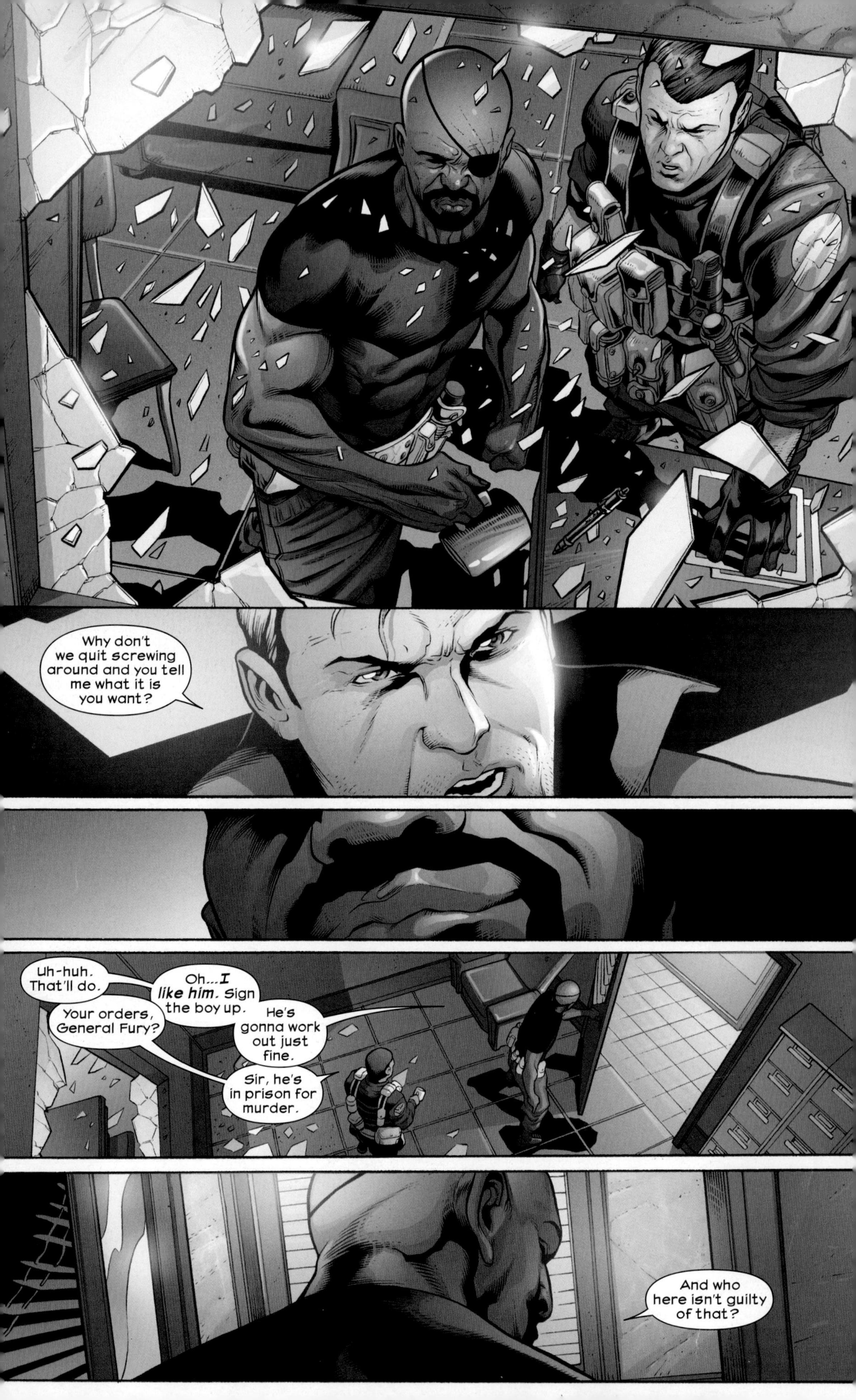

Why don't we quit screwing around and you tell me what it is you want?
Uh-huh. That'll do.
Oh... *I like him.* Sign the boy up.
Your orders, General Fury?
He's gonna work out just fine.
Sir, he's in prison for murder.
And who here isn't guilty of that?

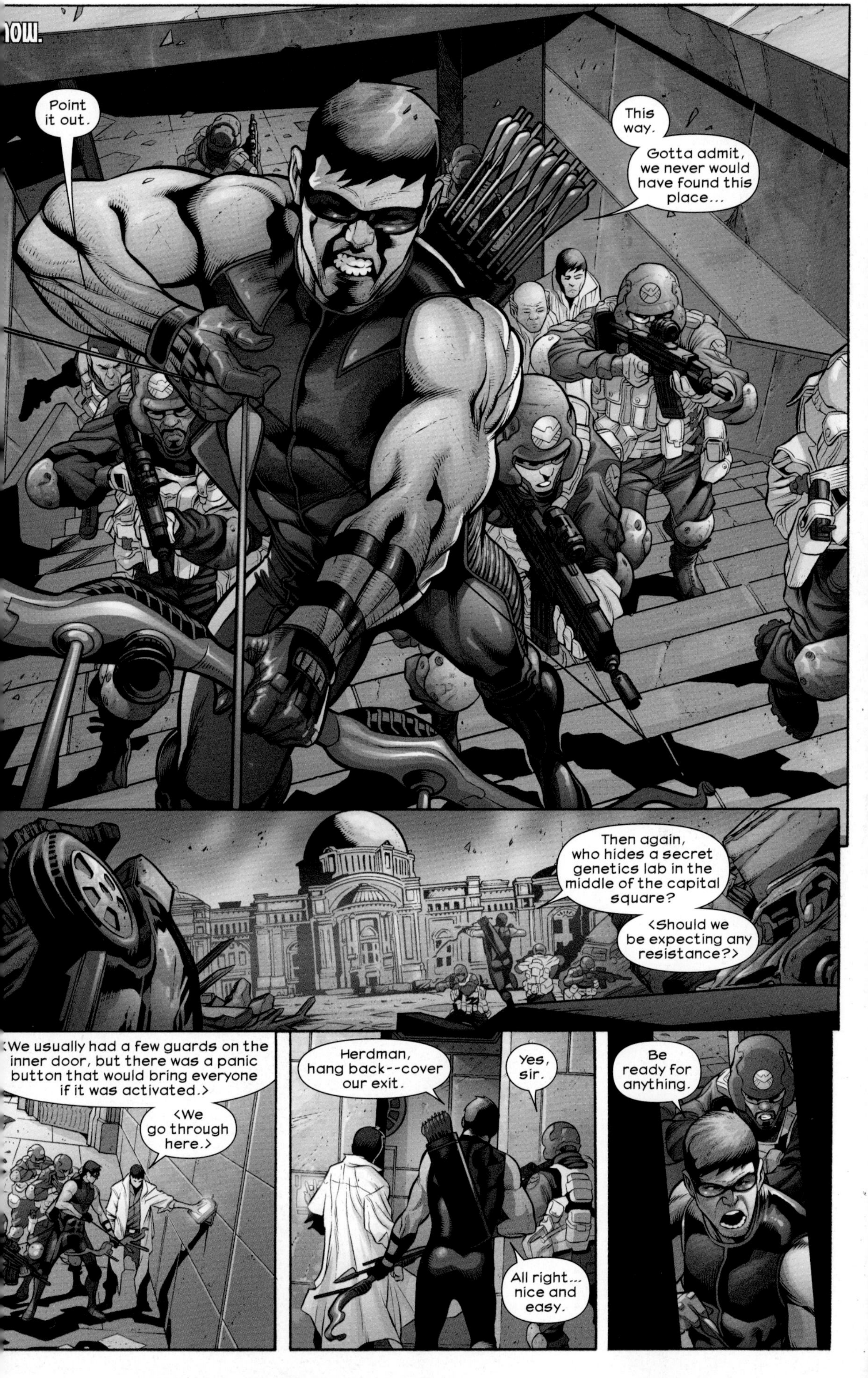
NOW.
Point it out.
This way.
Gotta admit, we never would have found this place...
Then again, who hides a secret genetics lab in the middle of the capital square?
<Should we be expecting any resistance?>
<We usually had a few guards on the inner door, but there was a panic button that would bring everyone if it was activated.>
<We go through here.>
Herdman, hang back--cover our exit.
Yes, sir.
All right... nice and easy.
Be ready for anything.

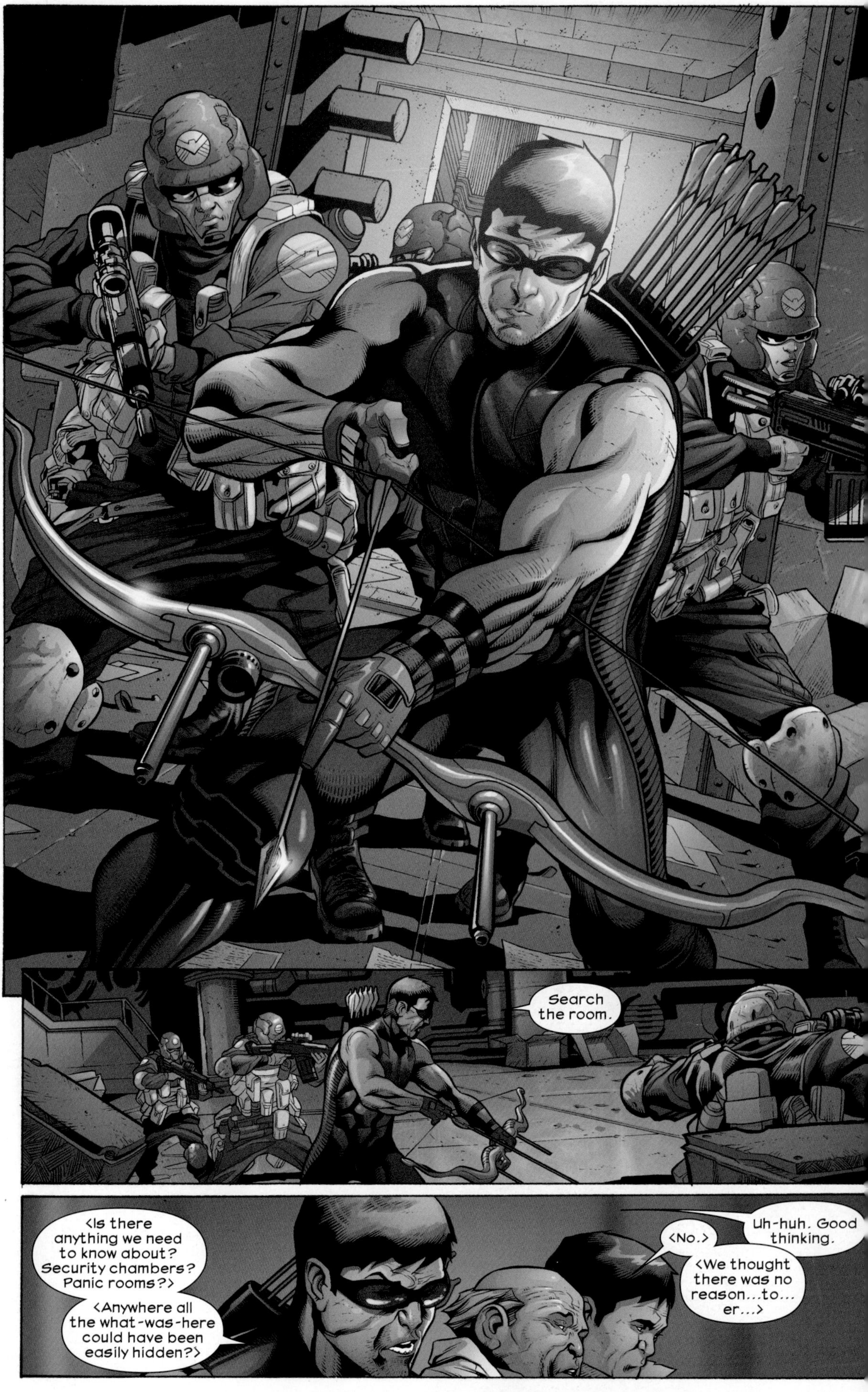
Search the room.
<Is there anything we need to know about? Security chambers? Panic rooms?>
<Anywhere all the what-was-here could have been easily hidden?>
<No.>
<We thought there was no reason...to... er...>
Uh-huh. Good thinking.

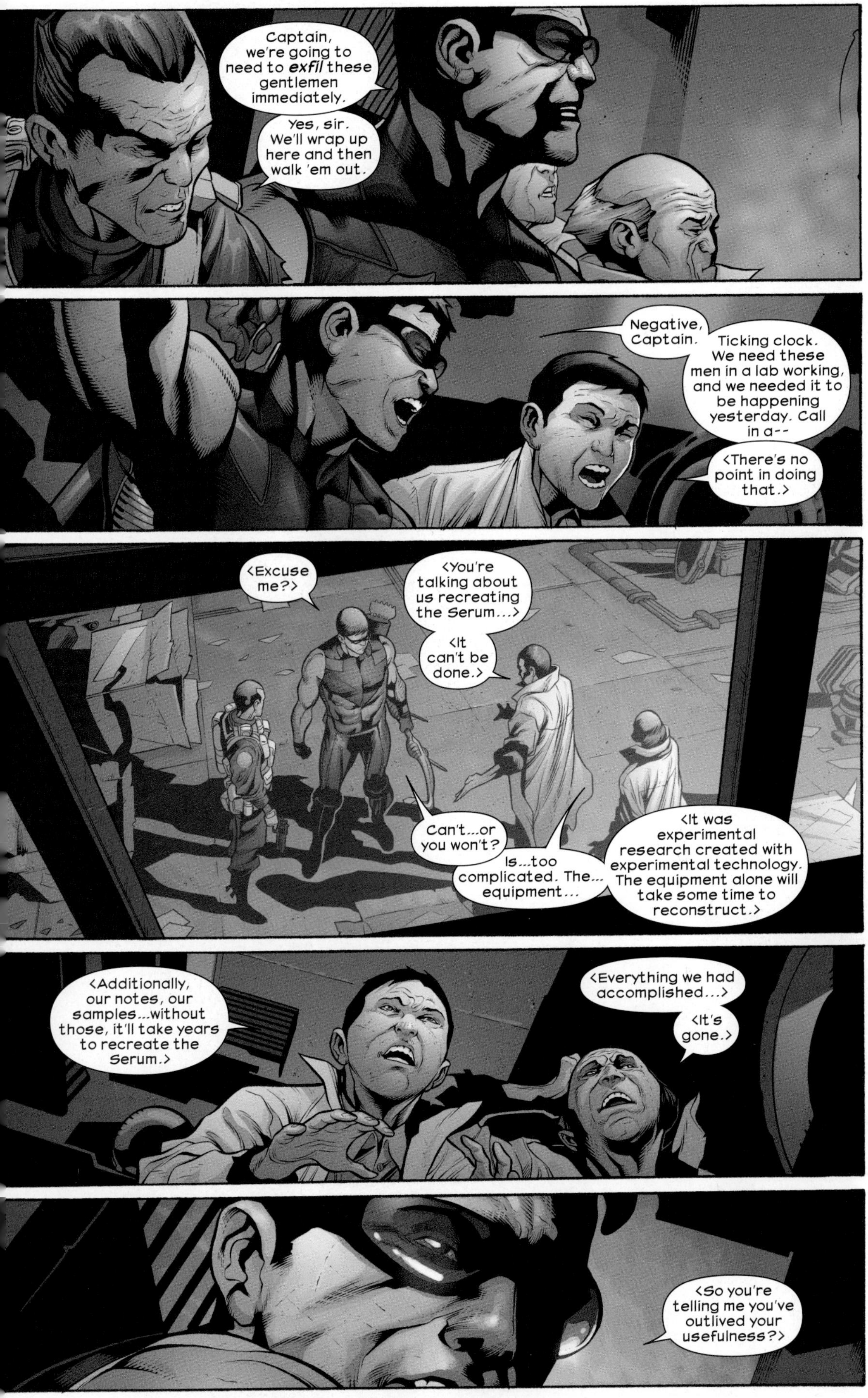
Captain, we're going to need to *exfil* these gentlemen immediately.
Yes, sir. We'll wrap up here and then walk 'em out.
Negative, Captain.
Ticking clock. We need these men in a lab working, and we needed it to be happening yesterday. Call in a--
<There's no point in doing that.>
<Excuse me?>
<You're talking about us recreating the Serum...>
<It can't be done.>
Can't...or you won't?
Is...too complicated. The... equipment...
<It was experimental research created with experimental technology. The equipment alone will take some time to reconstruct.>
<Additionally, our notes, our samples...without those, it'll take years to recreate the Serum.>
<Everything we had accomplished...>
<It's gone.>
<So you're telling me you've outlived your usefulness?>

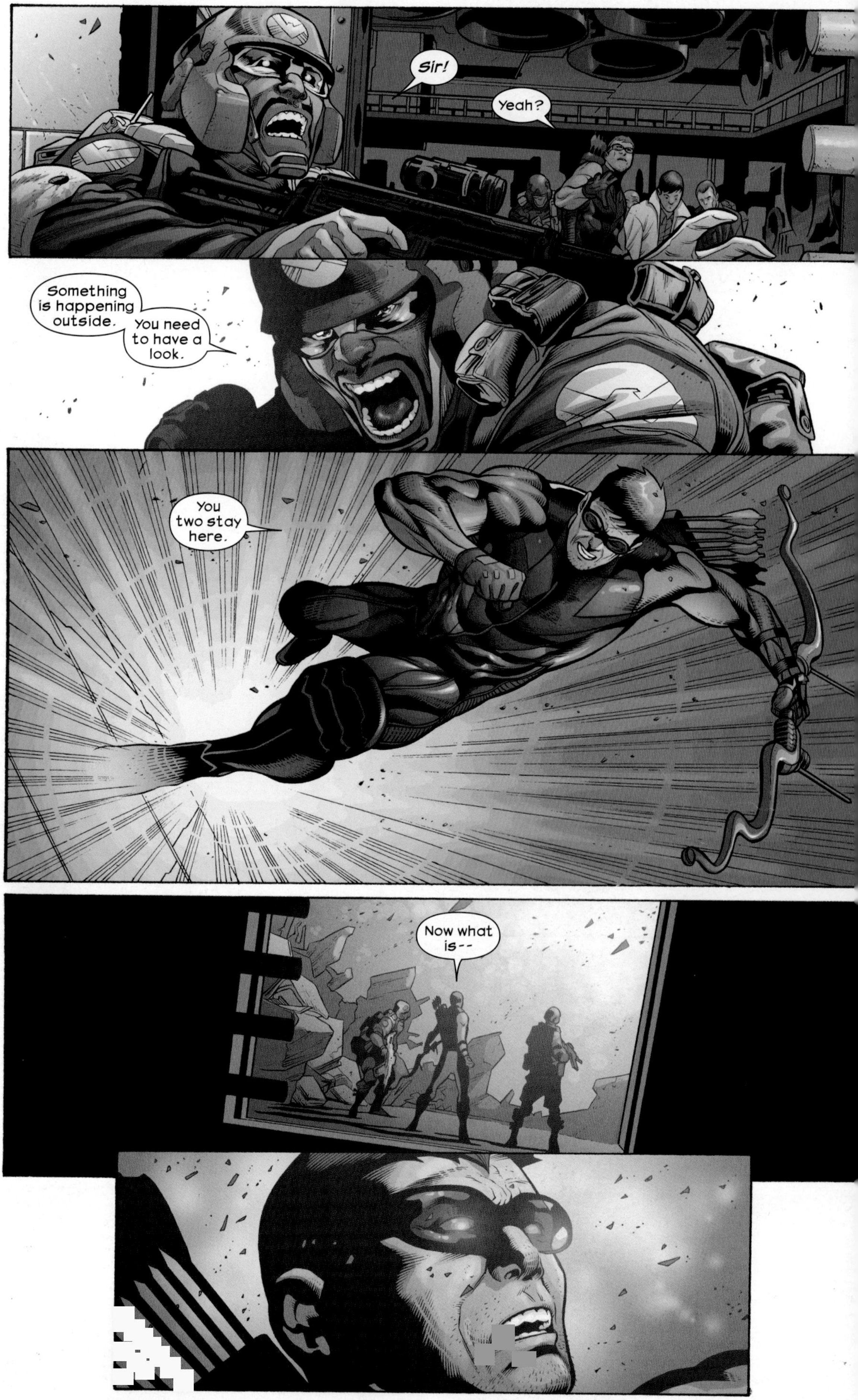
Sir!
Yeah?
Something is happening outside.
You need to have a look.
You two stay here.
Now what is--

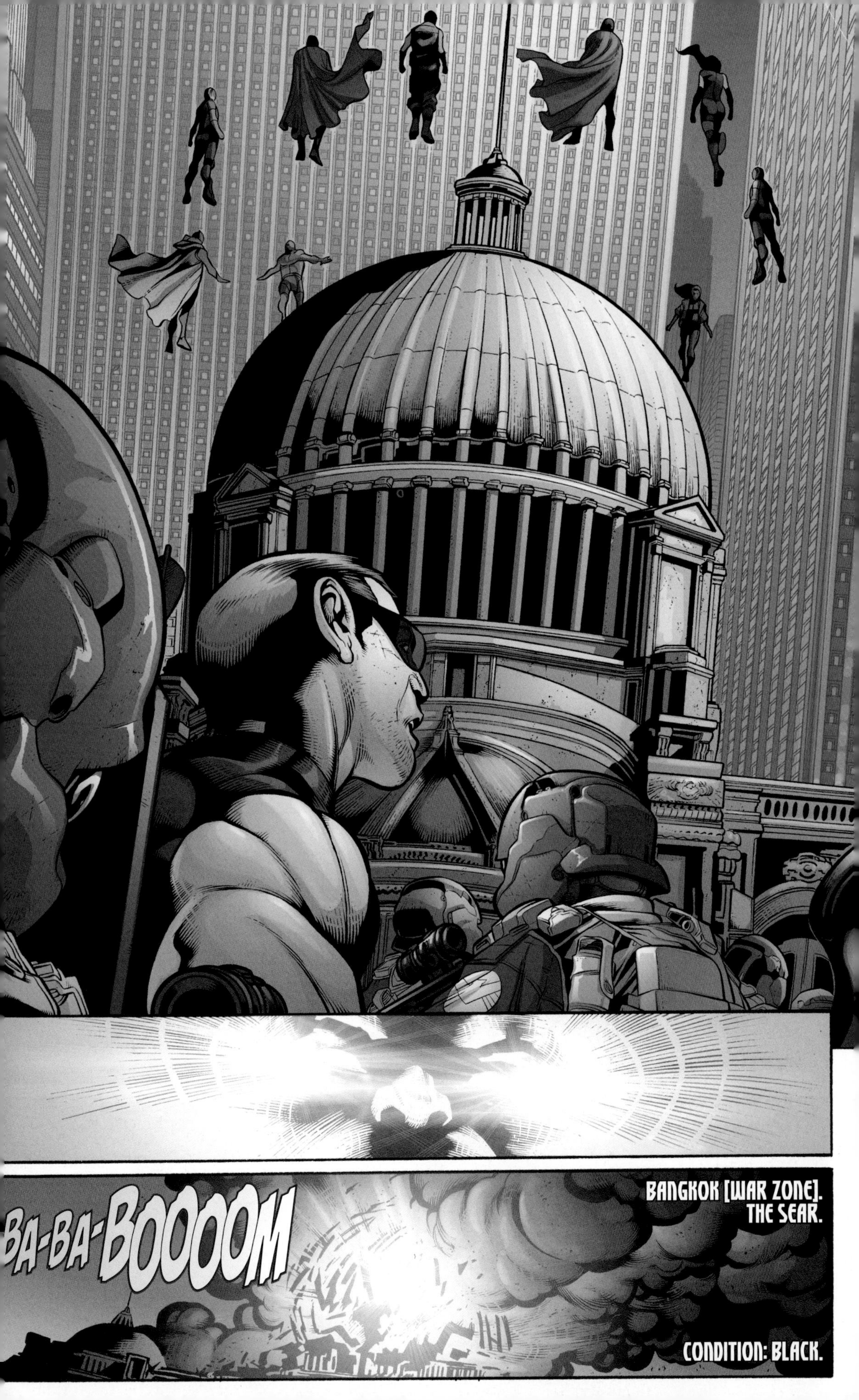
BA-BA-BOOOOM
BANGKOK [WAR ZONE].
THE SEAR.
CONDITION: BLACK.

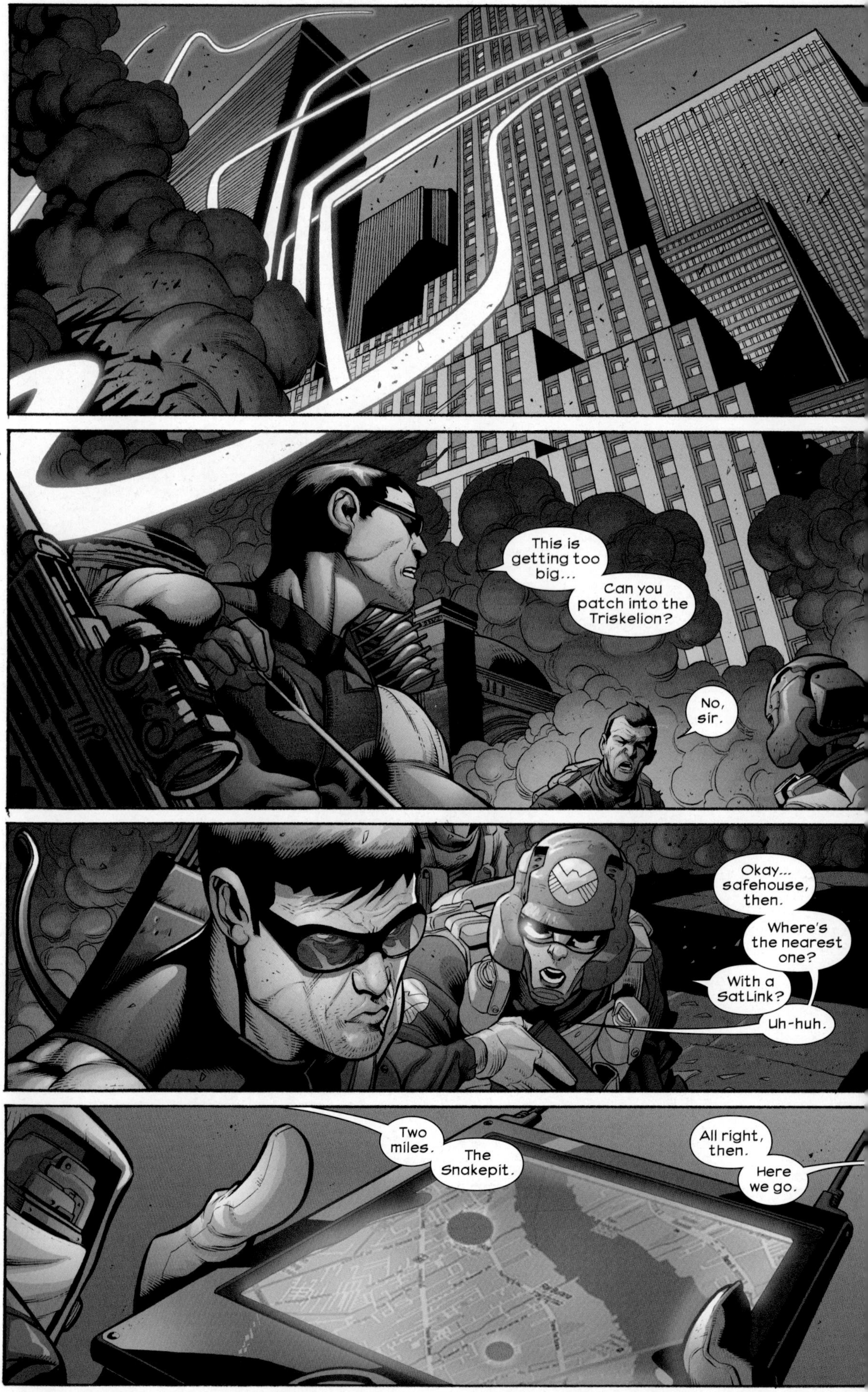
This is getting too big...
Can you patch into the Triskelion?
No, sir.
Okay... safehouse, then.
Where's the nearest one?
With a SatLink?
Uh-huh.
Two miles.
The Snakepit.
All right, then.
Here we go.

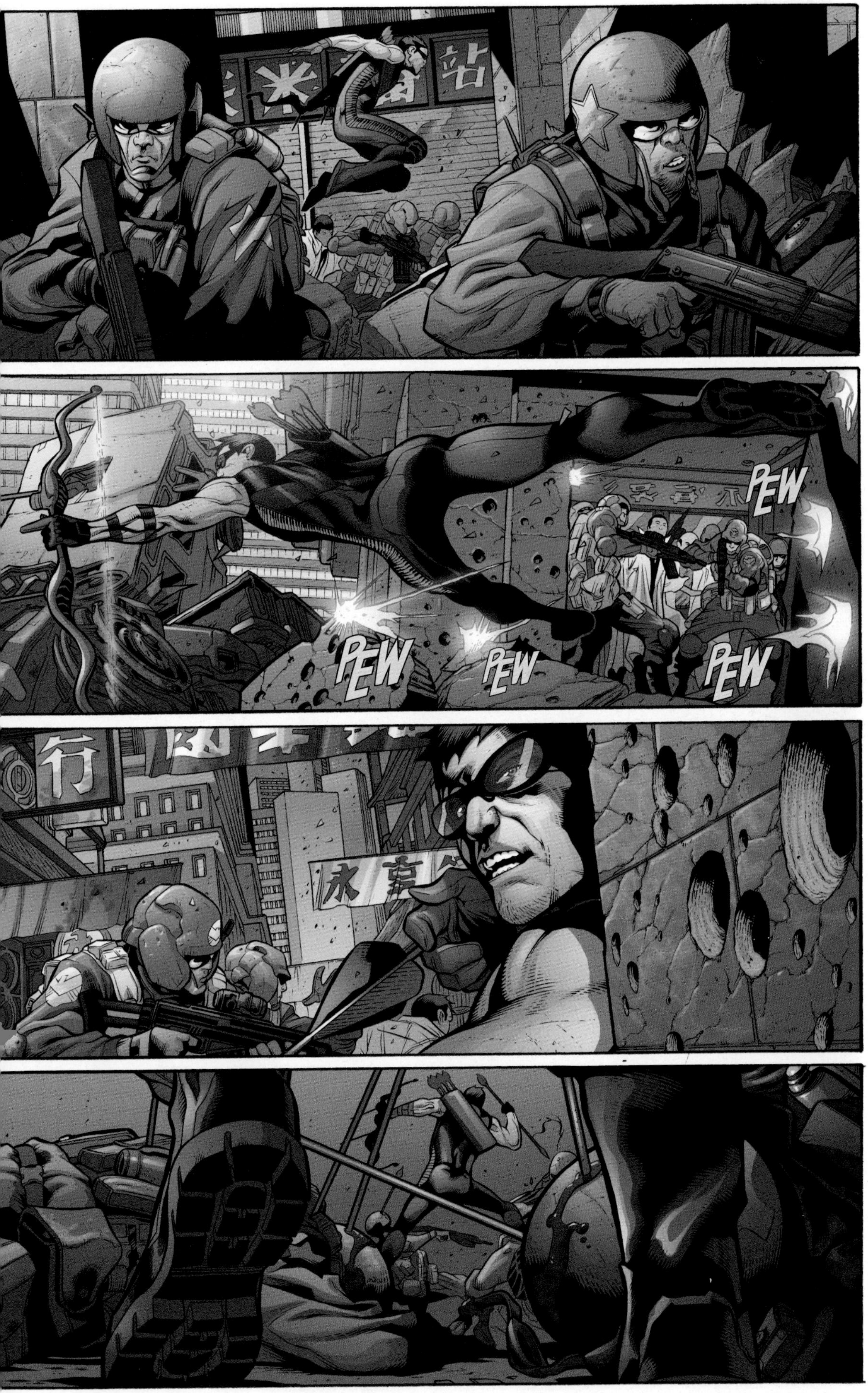
PEW
PEW
PEW
PEW

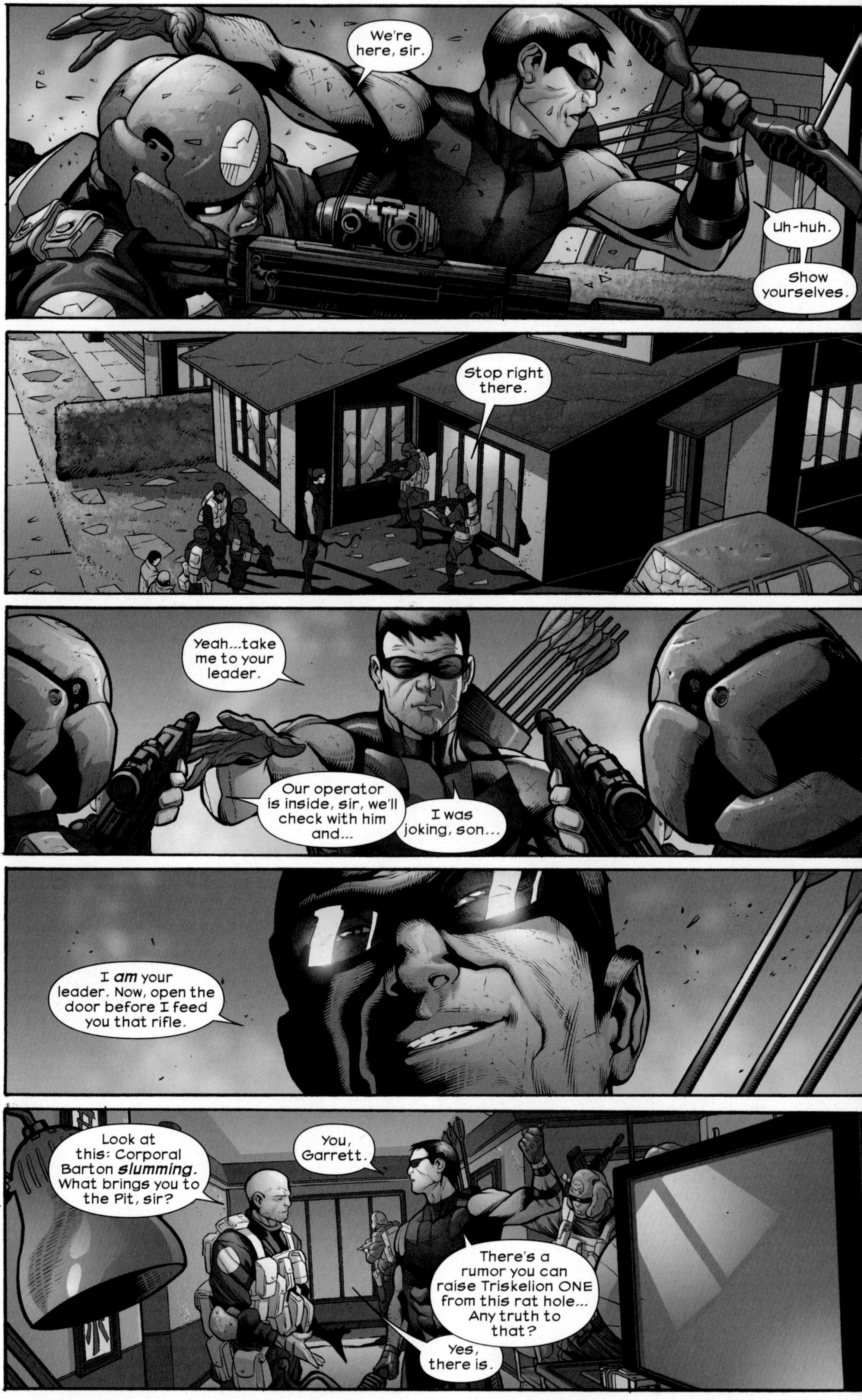
We're here, sir.
Uh-huh.
Show yourselves.
Stop right there.
Yeah...take me to your leader.
Our operator is inside, sir, we'll check with him and...
I was joking, son...
I *am* your leader. Now, open the door before I feed you that rifle.
Look at this: Corporal Barton *slumming.* What brings you to the Pit, sir?
You, Garrett.
There's a rumor you can raise Triskelion ONE from this rat hole... Any truth to that?
Yes, there is.

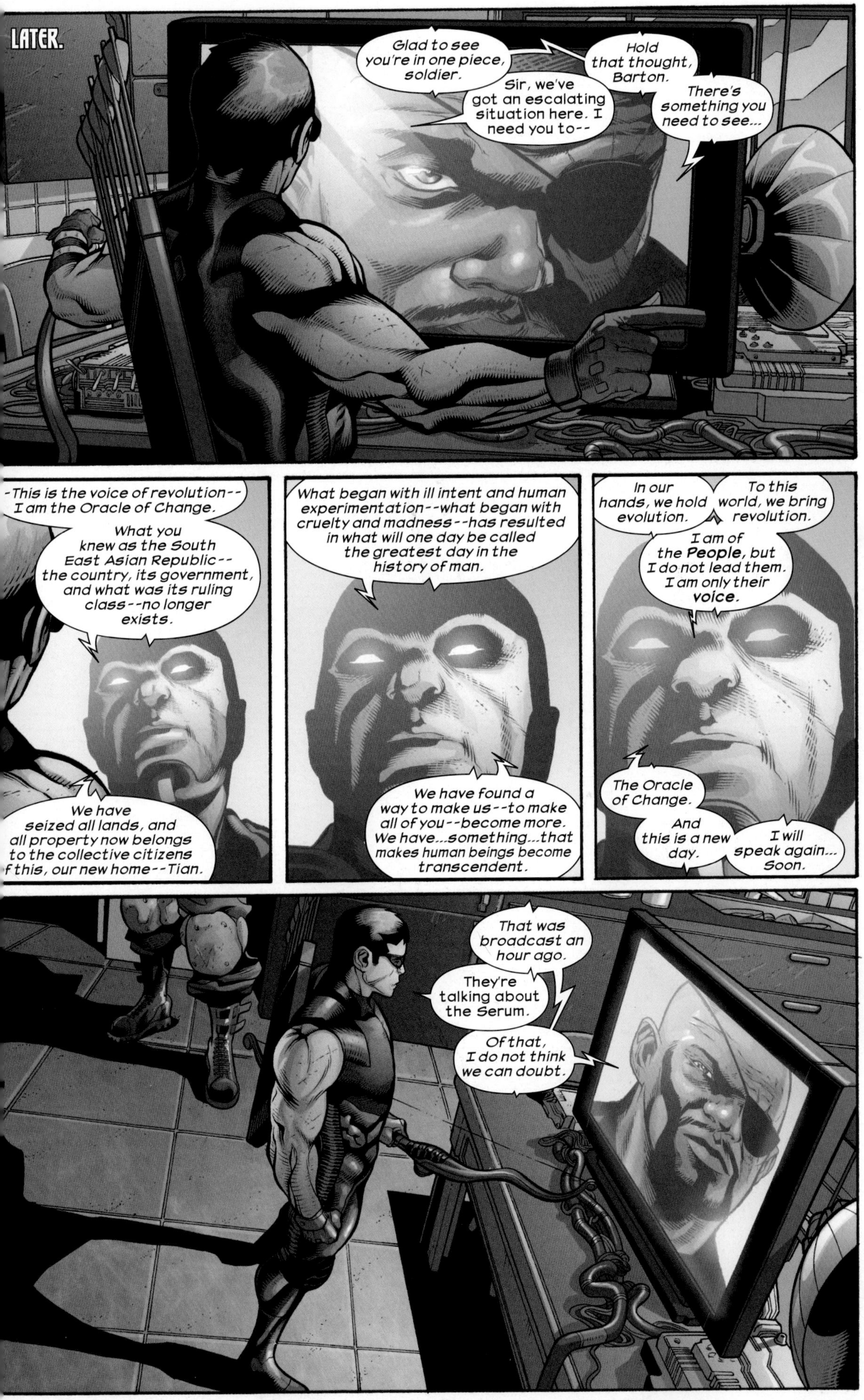
LATER.
Glad to see you're in one piece, soldier.
Sir, we've got an escalating situation here. I need you to--
Hold that thought, Barton.
There's something you need to see...
-This is the voice of revolution-- I am the Oracle of Change.
What you knew as the South East Asian Republic-- the country, its government, and what was its ruling class--no longer exists.
We have seized all lands, and all property now belongs to the collective citizens f this, our new home--Tian.
What began with ill intent and human experimentation--what began with cruelty and madness--has resulted in what will one day be called the greatest day in the history of man.
We have found a way to make us--to make all of you--become more. We have...something...that makes human beings become transcendent.
In our hands, we hold evolution.
To this world, we bring revolution.
I am of the **People**, but I do not lead them. I am only their **voice.**
The Oracle of Change.
And this is a new day.
I will speak again... Soon.
That was broadcast an hour ago.
They're talking about the Serum.
Of that, I do not think we can doubt.

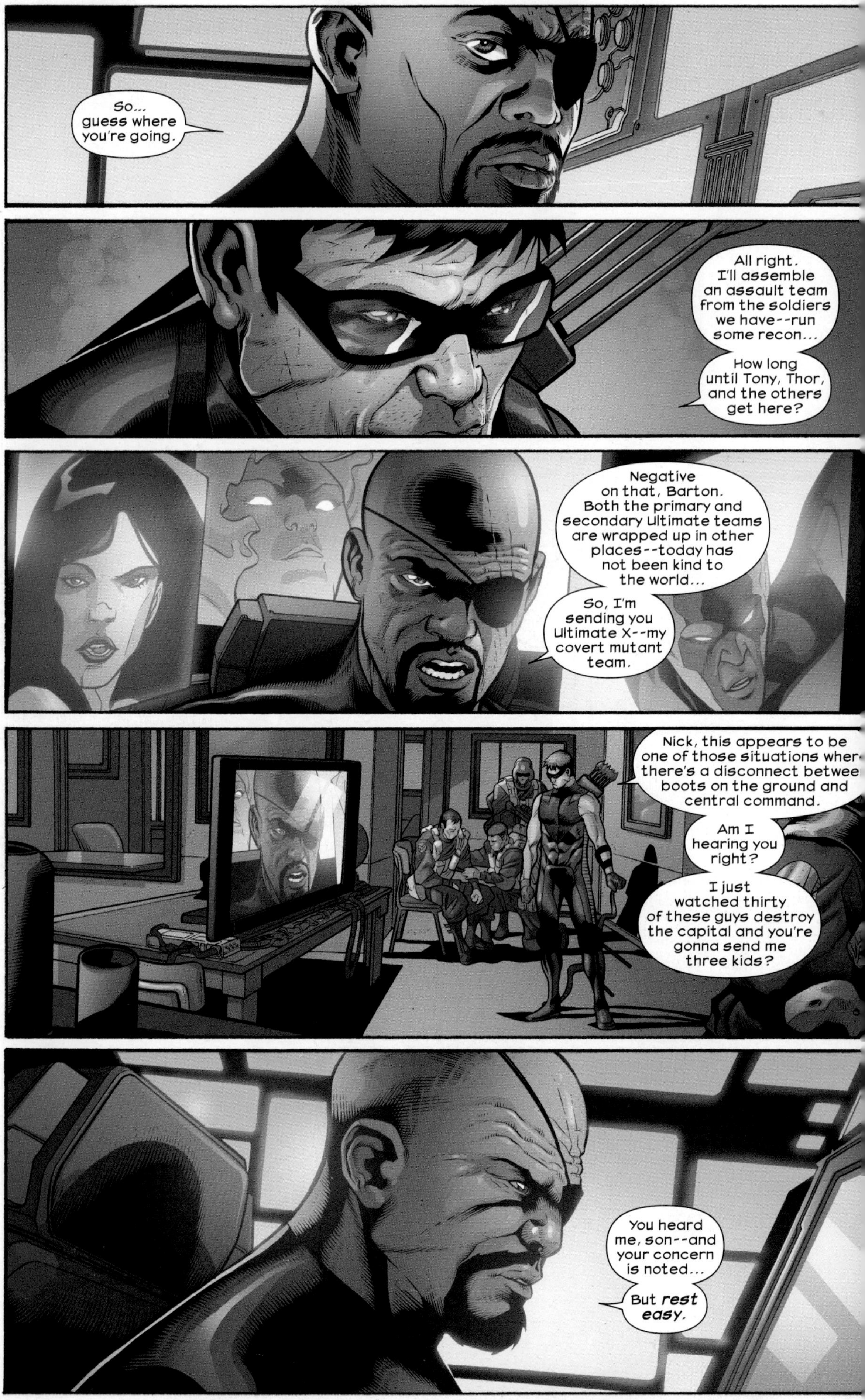

So... guess where you're going.
All right. I'll assemble an assault team from the soldiers we have--run some recon...
How long until Tony, Thor, and the others get here?
Negative on that, Barton. Both the primary and secondary Ultimate teams are wrapped up in other places--today has not been kind to the world...
So, I'm sending you Ultimate X--my covert mutant team.
Nick, this appears to be one of those situations wher there's a disconnect betwee boots on the ground and central command.
Am I hearing you right?
I just watched thirty of these guys destroy the capital and you're gonna send me three kids?
You heard me, son--and your concern is noted...
But *rest easy.*

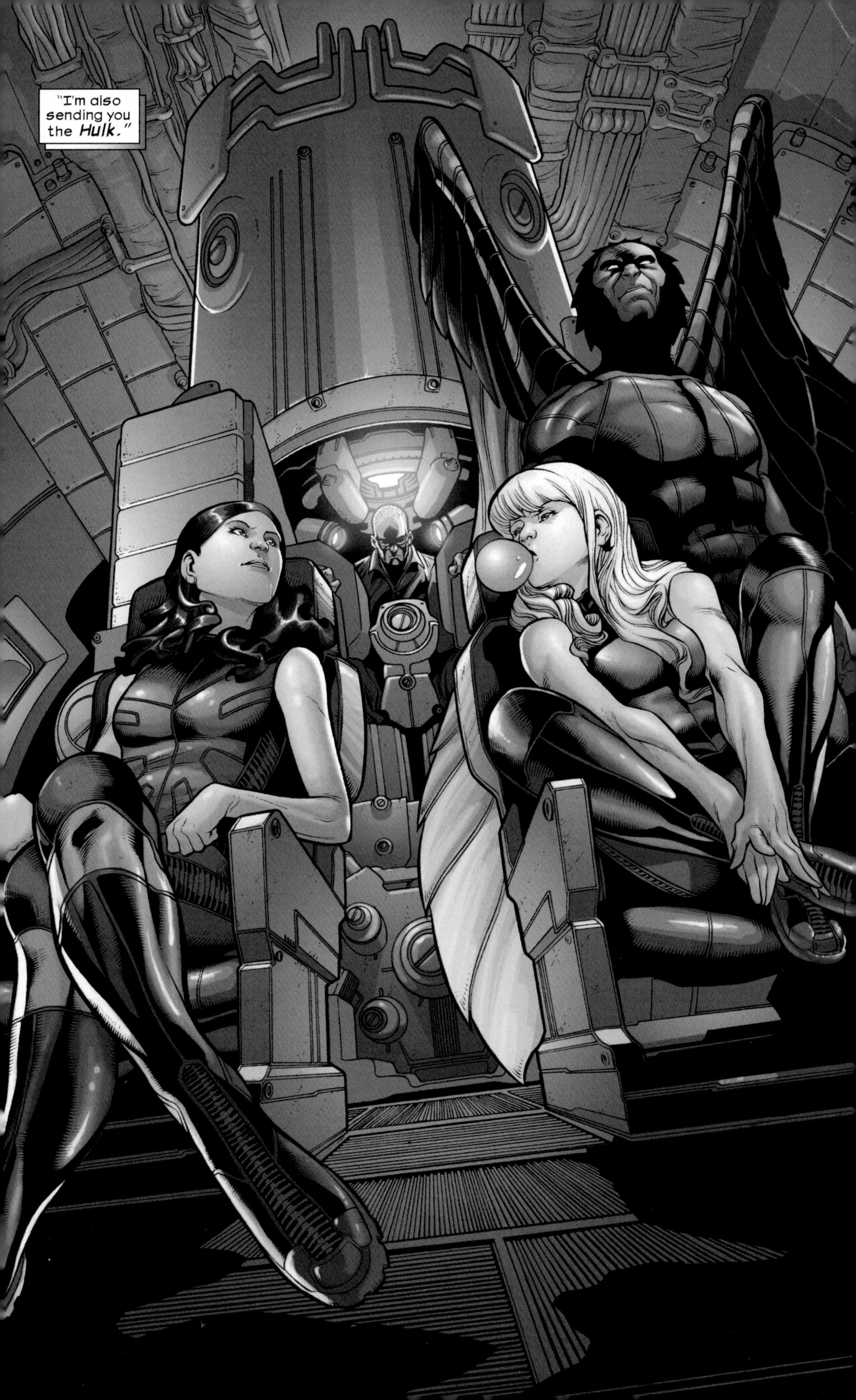
"I'm also sending you the *Hulk.*"

3

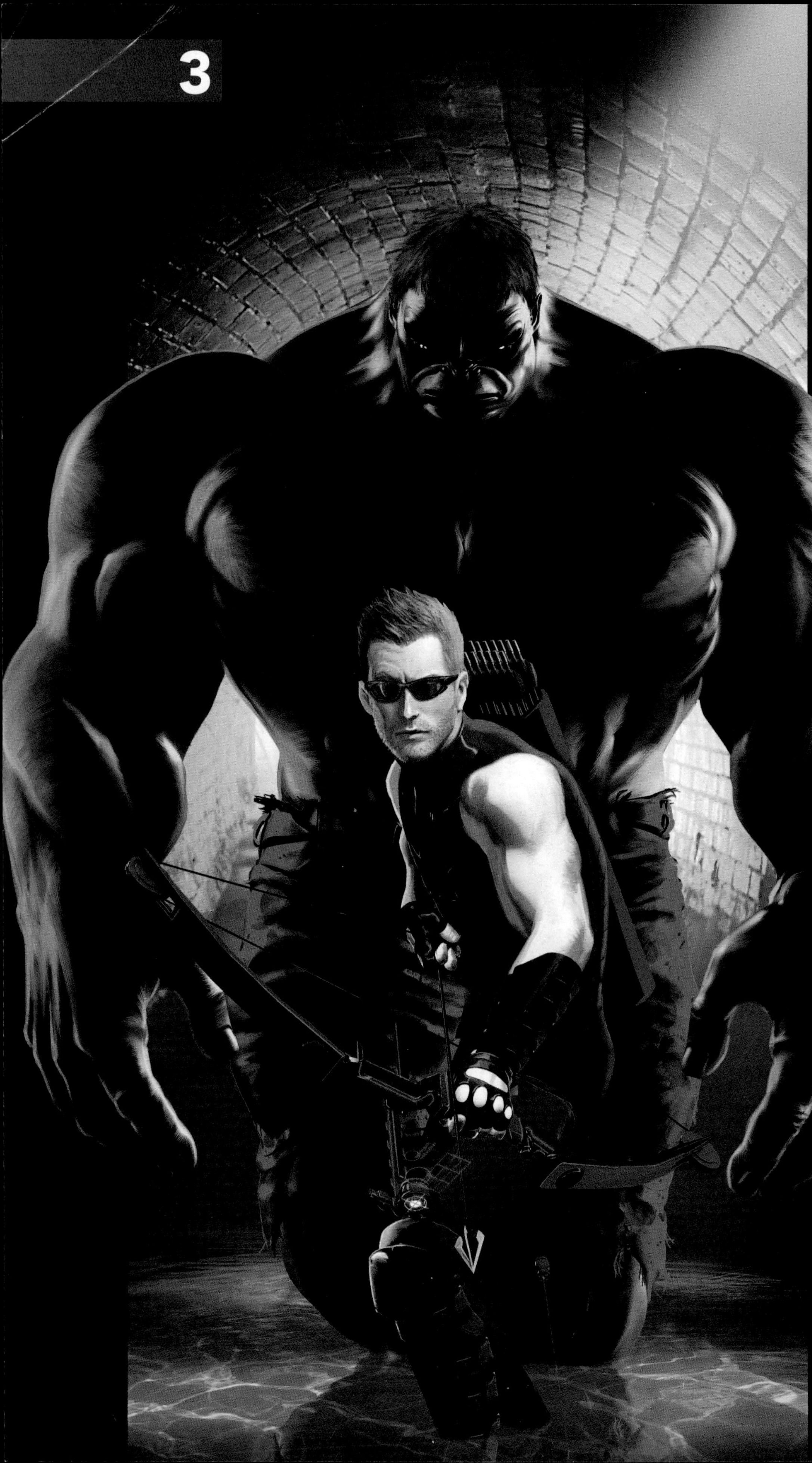

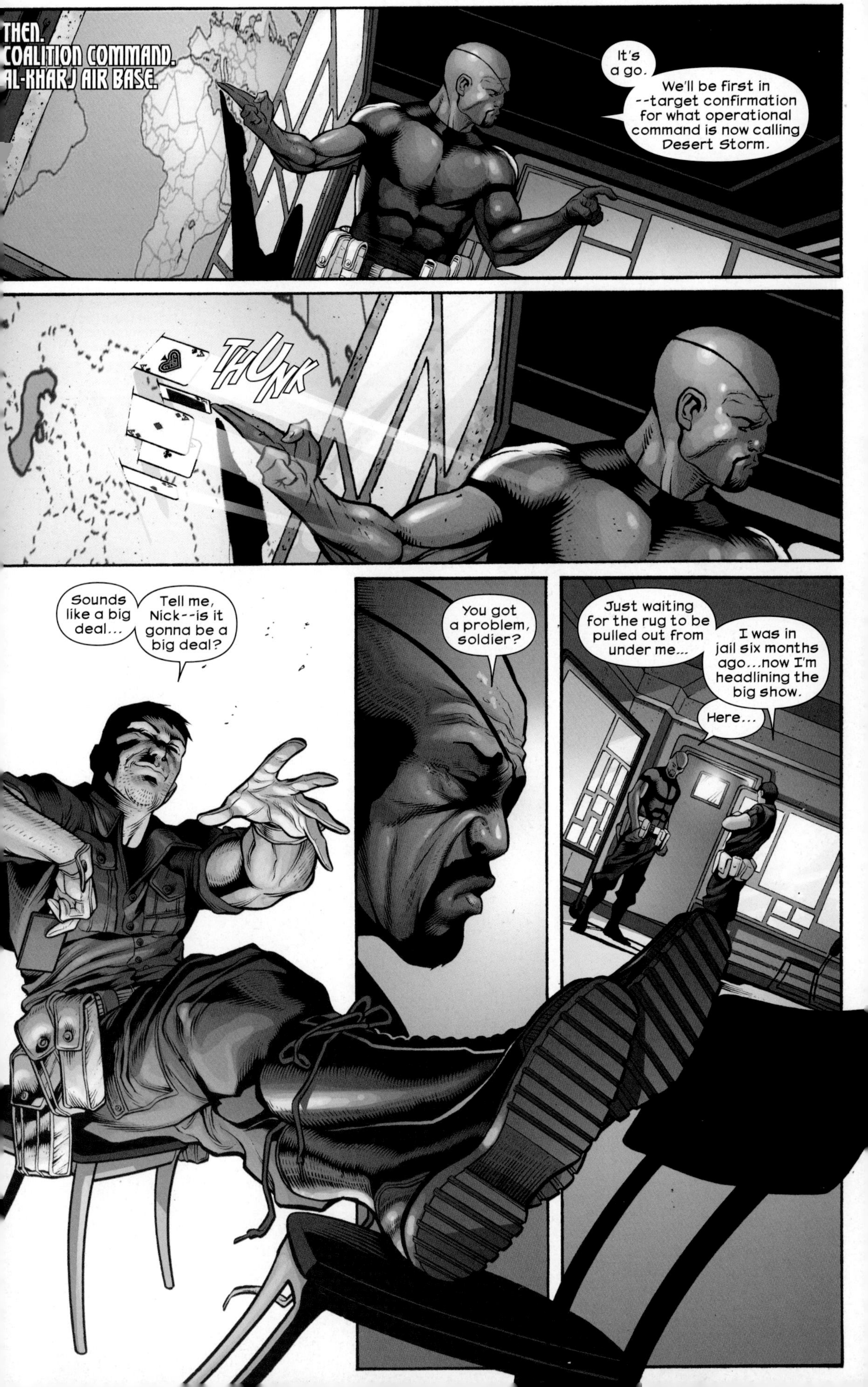
THEN.
COALITION COMMAND.
AL-KHARJ AIR BASE.
It's a go.
We'll be first in --target confirmation for what operational command is now calling Desert Storm.
THUNK
Sounds like a big deal...
Tell me, Nick--is it gonna be a big deal?
You got a problem, soldier?
Just waiting for the rug to be pulled out from under me...
I was in jail six months ago...now I'm headlining the big show.
Here...

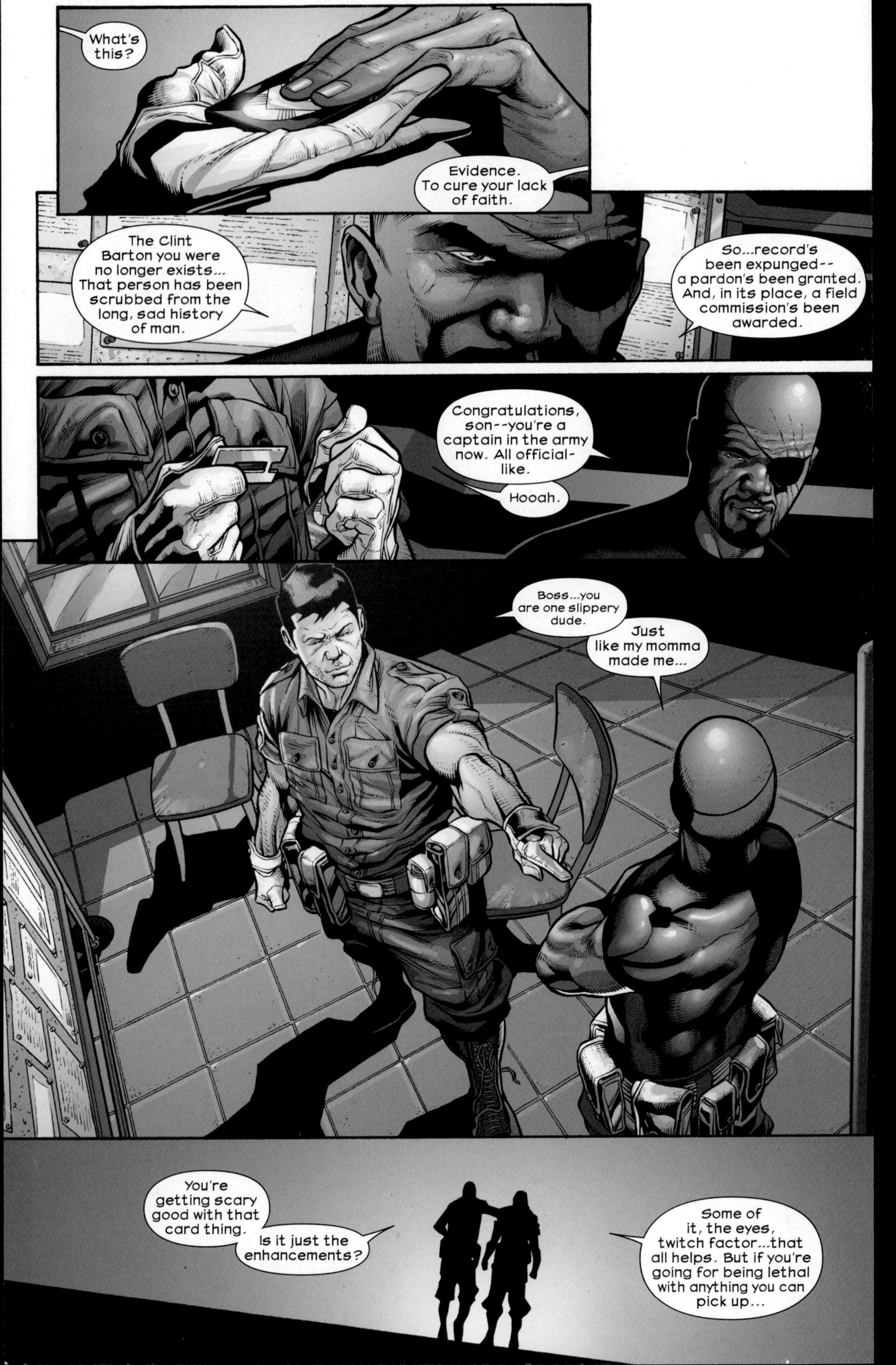
What's this?
Evidence. To cure your lack of faith.
The Clint Barton you were no longer exists... That person has been scrubbed from the long, sad history of man.
So...record's been expunged-- a pardon's been granted. And, in its place, a field commission's been awarded.
Congratulations, son--you're a captain in the army now. All official-like.
Hooah.
Boss...you are one slippery dude.
Just like my momma made me...
You're getting scary good with that card thing.
Is it just the enhancements?
Some of it, the eyes, twitch factor...that all helps. But if you're going for being lethal with anything you can pick up...

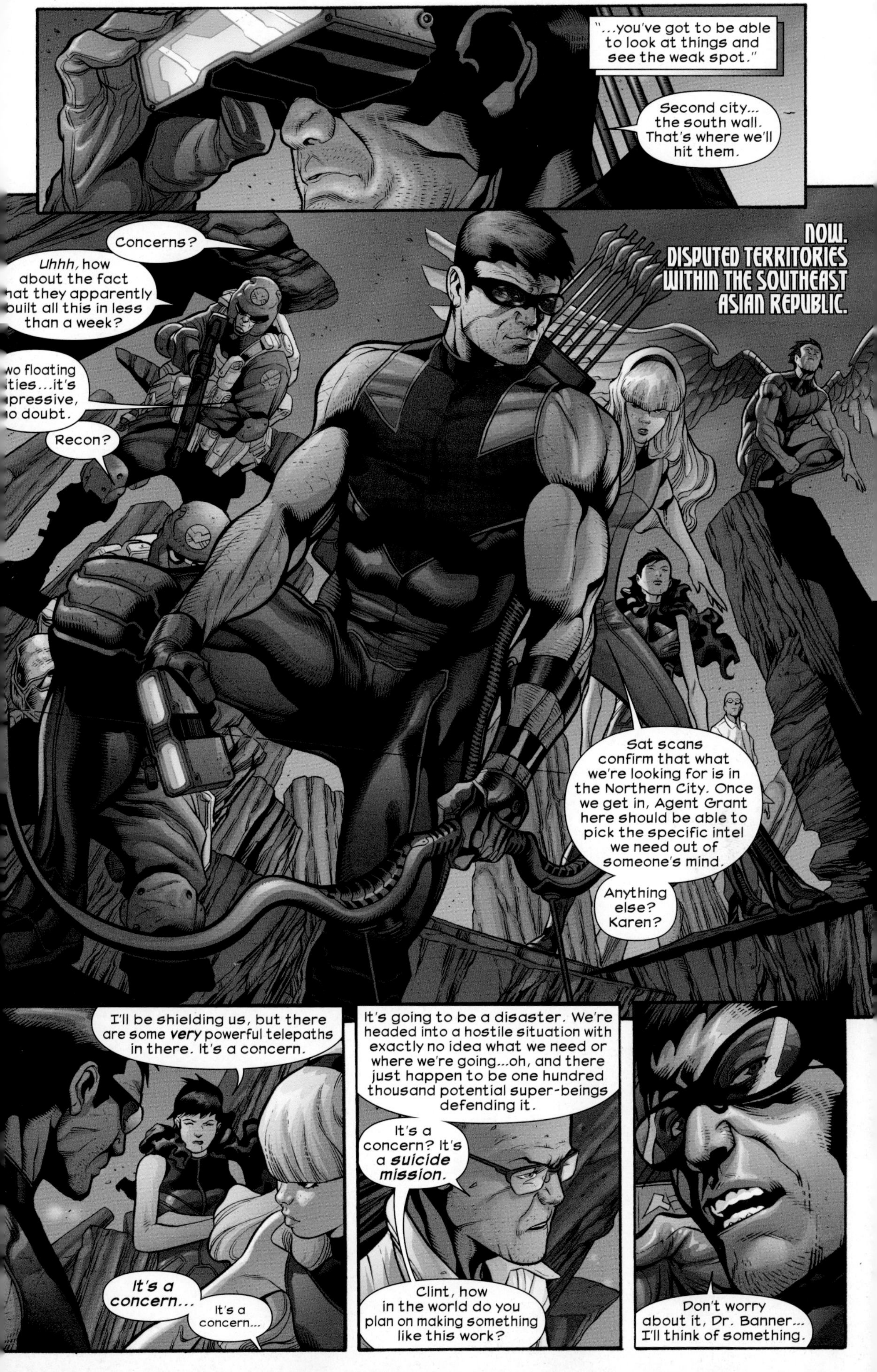

"...you've got to be able to look at things and see the weak spot."
Second city... the south wall. That's where we'll hit them.
NOW. DISPUTED TERRITORIES WITHIN THE SOUTHEAST ASIAN REPUBLIC.
Concerns?
Uhhh, how about the fact hat they apparently built all this in less than a week?
wo floating ities...it's pressive, o doubt.
Recon?
Sat scans confirm that what we're looking for is in the Northern City. Once we get in, Agent Grant here should be able to pick the specific intel we need out of someone's mind.
Anything else? Karen?
I'll be shielding us, but there are some very powerful telepaths in there. It's a concern.
It's a concern...
It's a concern...
It's going to be a disaster. We're headed into a hostile situation with exactly no idea what we need or where we're going...oh, and there just happen to be one hundred thousand potential super-beings defending it.
It's a concern? It's a suicide mission.
Clint, how in the world do you plan on making something like this work?
Don't worry about it, Dr. Banner... I'll think of something.

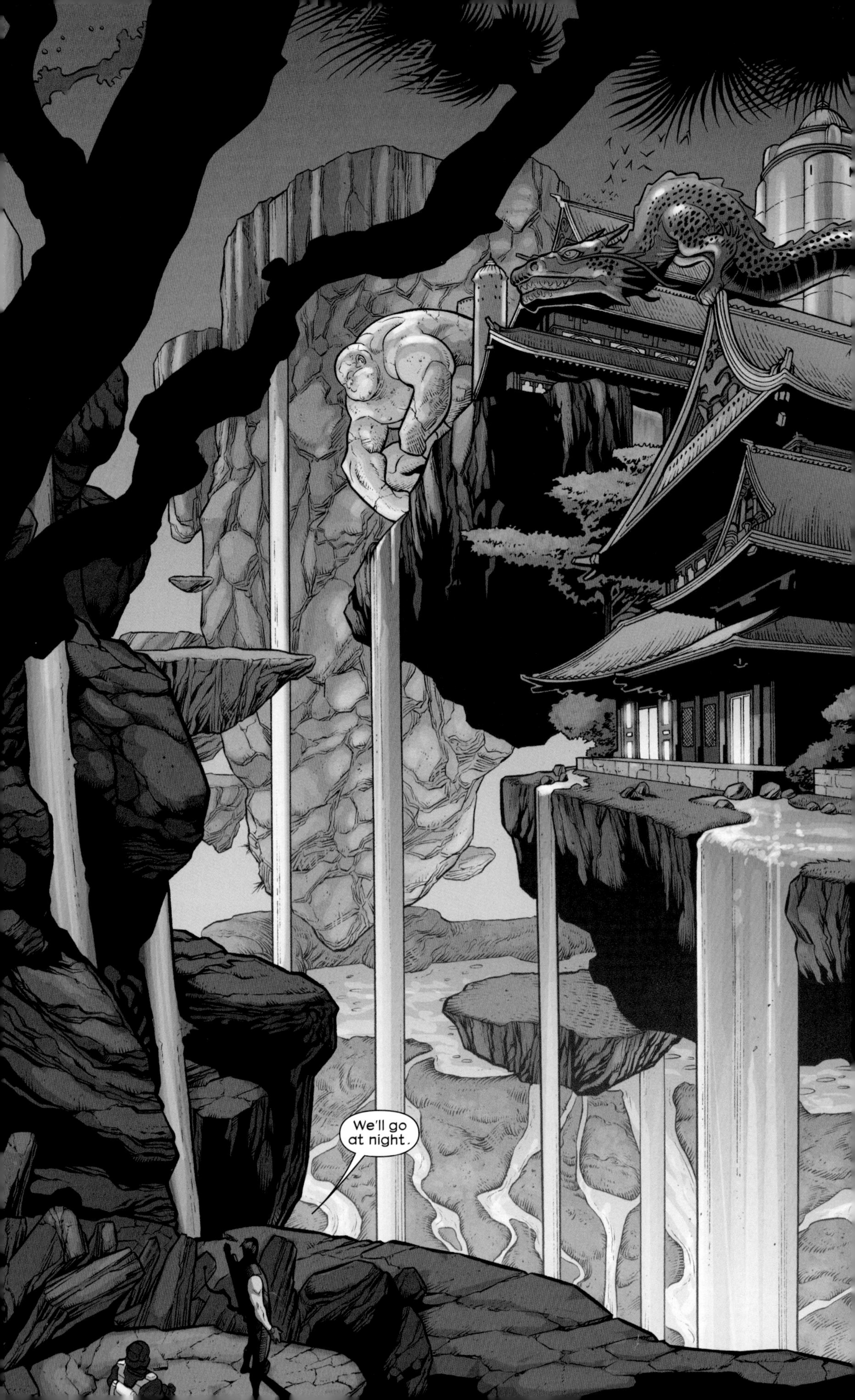
We'll go at night.

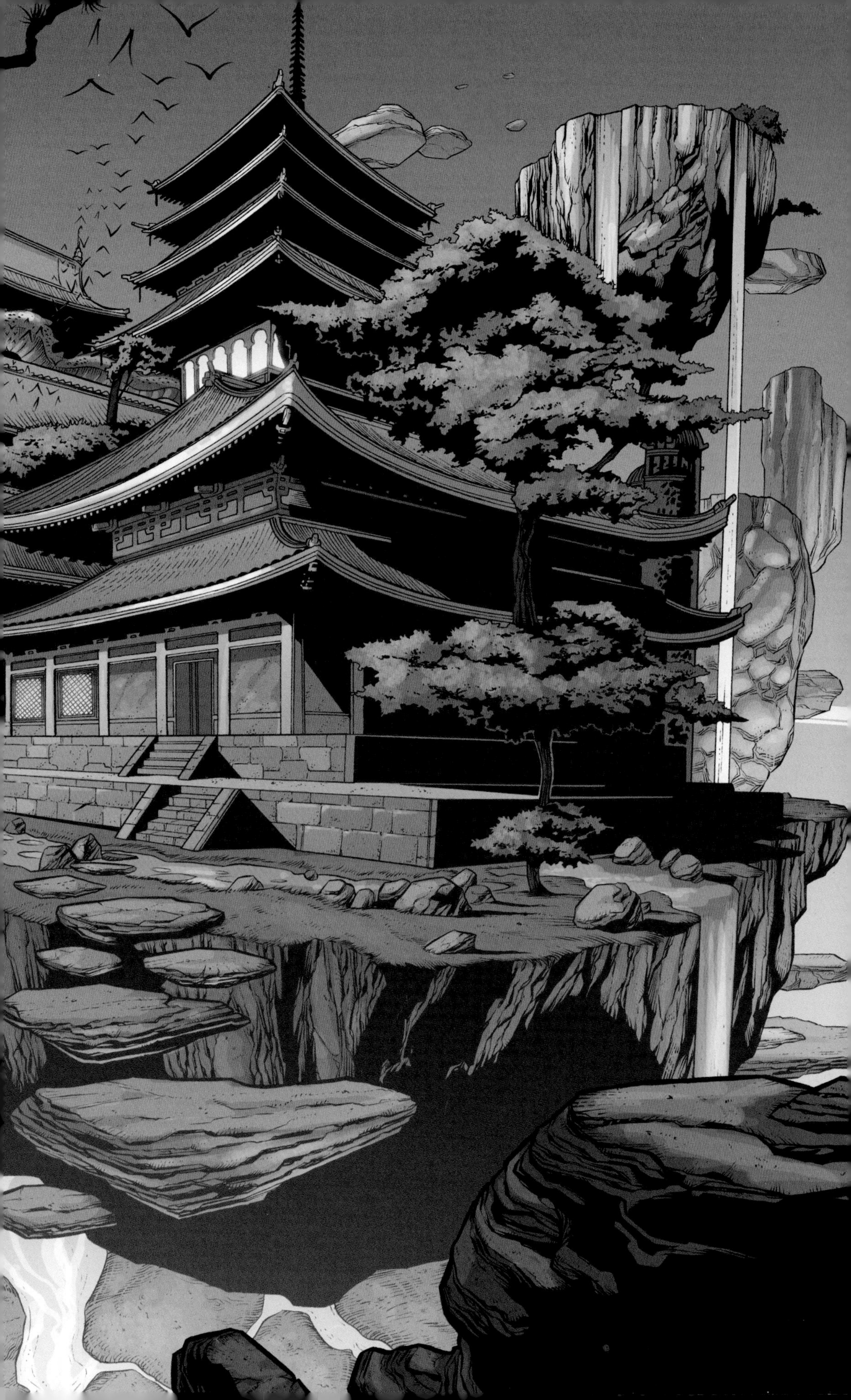

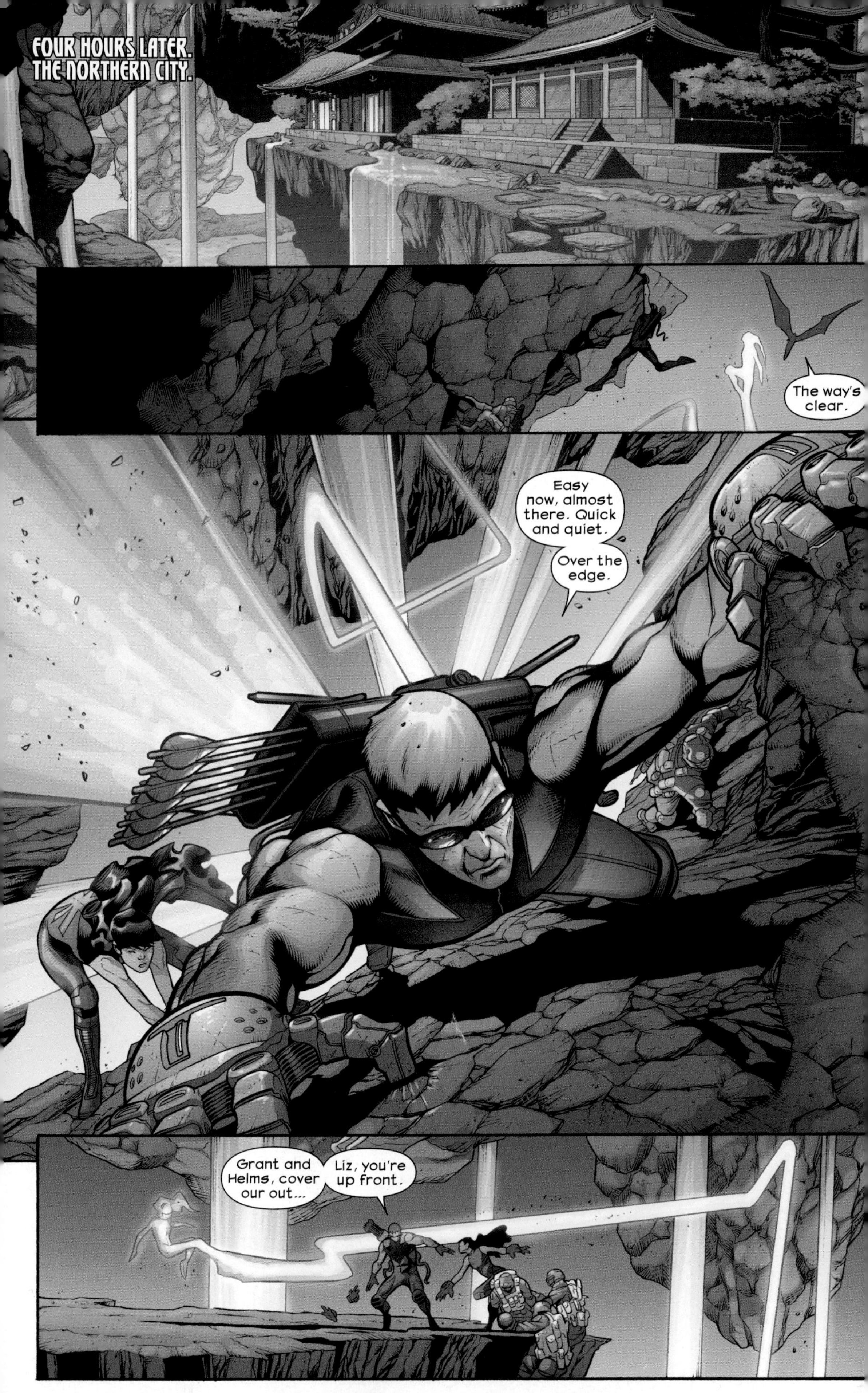
FOUR HOURS LATER.
THE NORTHERN CITY.
The way's clear.
Easy now, almost there. Quick and quiet.
Over the edge.
Grant and Helms, cover our out...
Liz, you're up front.

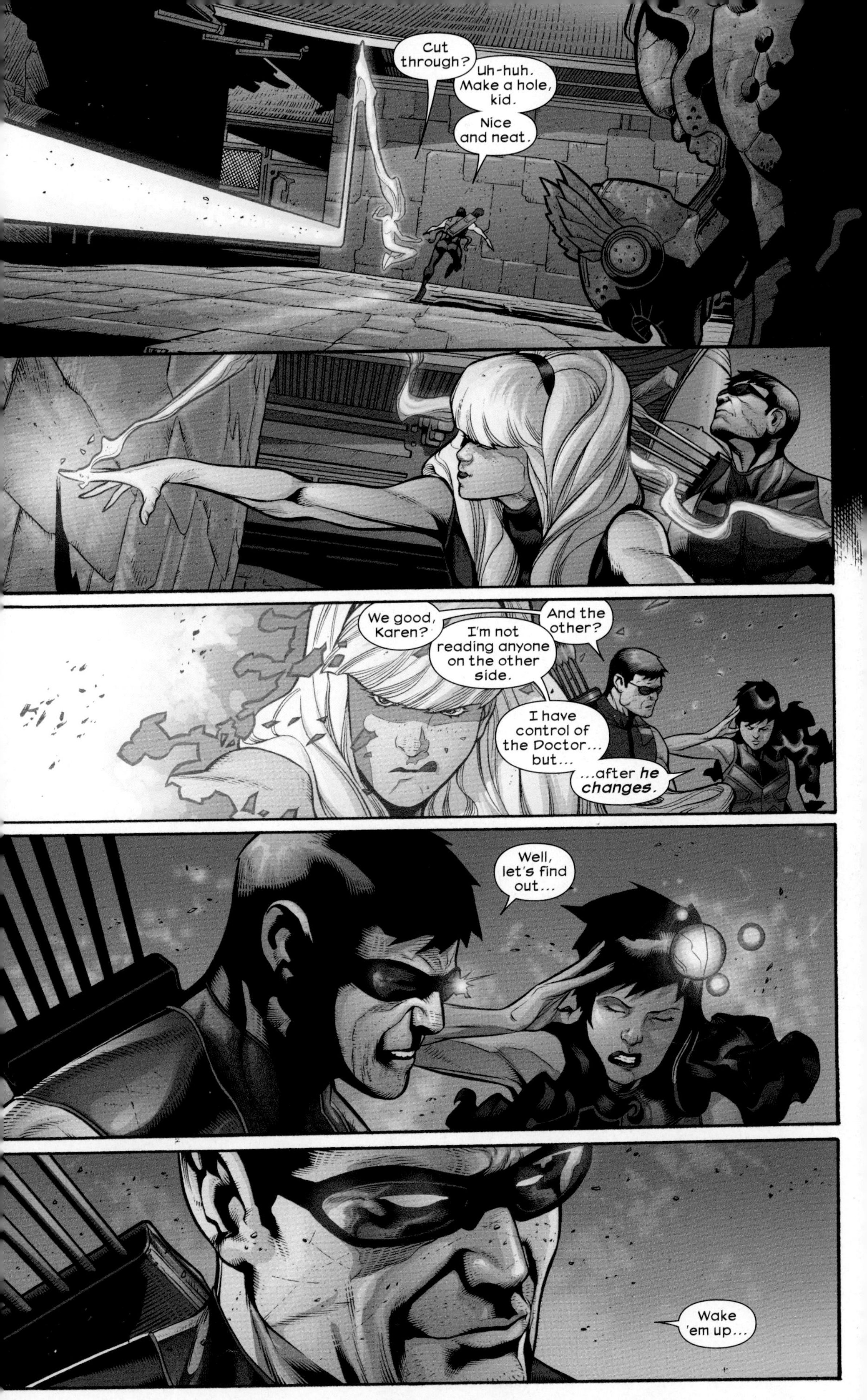
Cut through?
Uh-huh. Make a hole, kid.
Nice and neat.
We good, Karen?
I'm not reading anyone on the other side.
And the other?
I have control of the Doctor... but...
...after he changes.
Well, let's find out...
Wake 'em up...

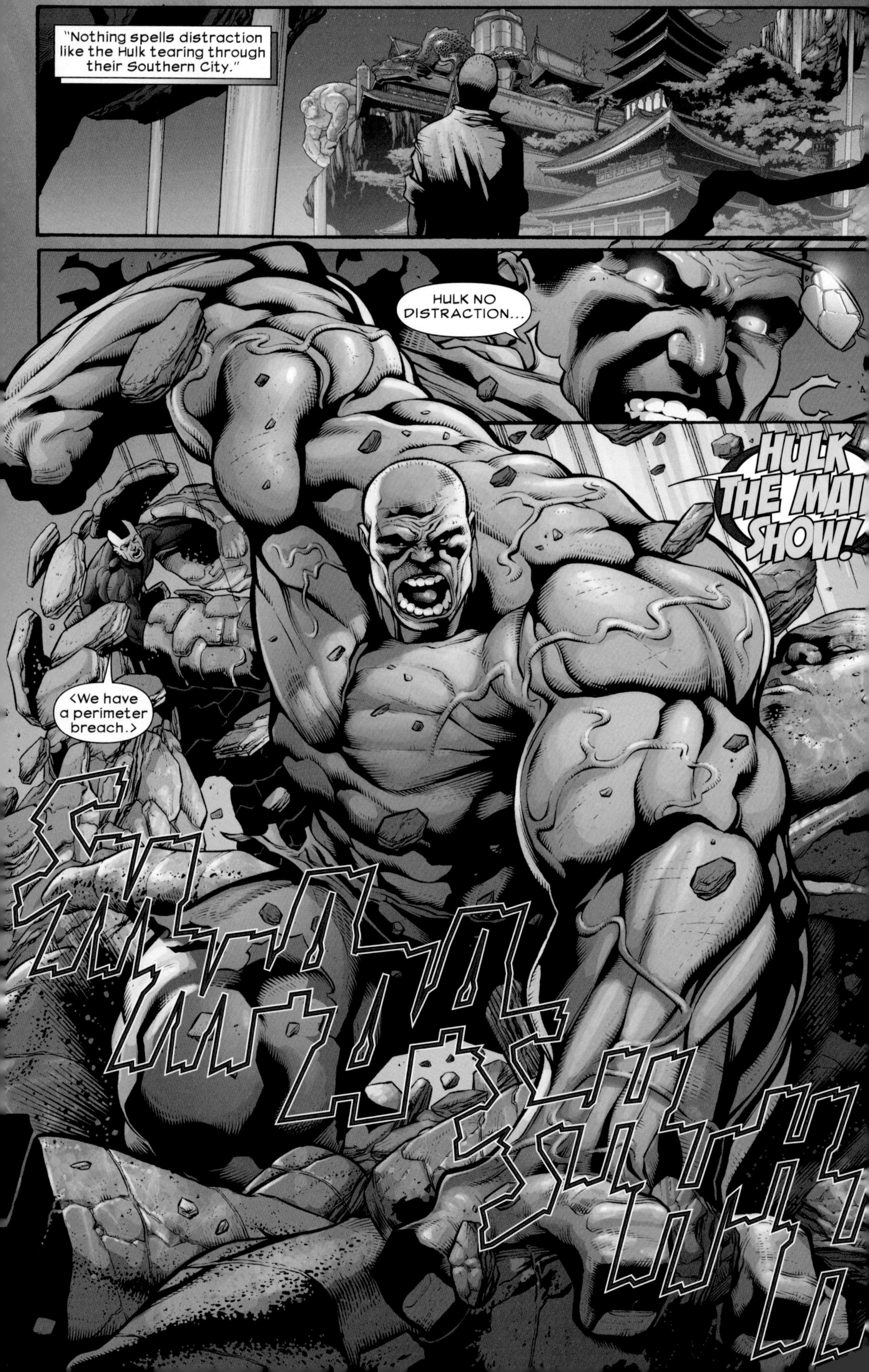
"Nothing spells distraction like the Hulk tearing through their Southern City."
HULK NO DISTRACTION...
HULK THE MAI SHOW!
<We have a perimeter breach.>

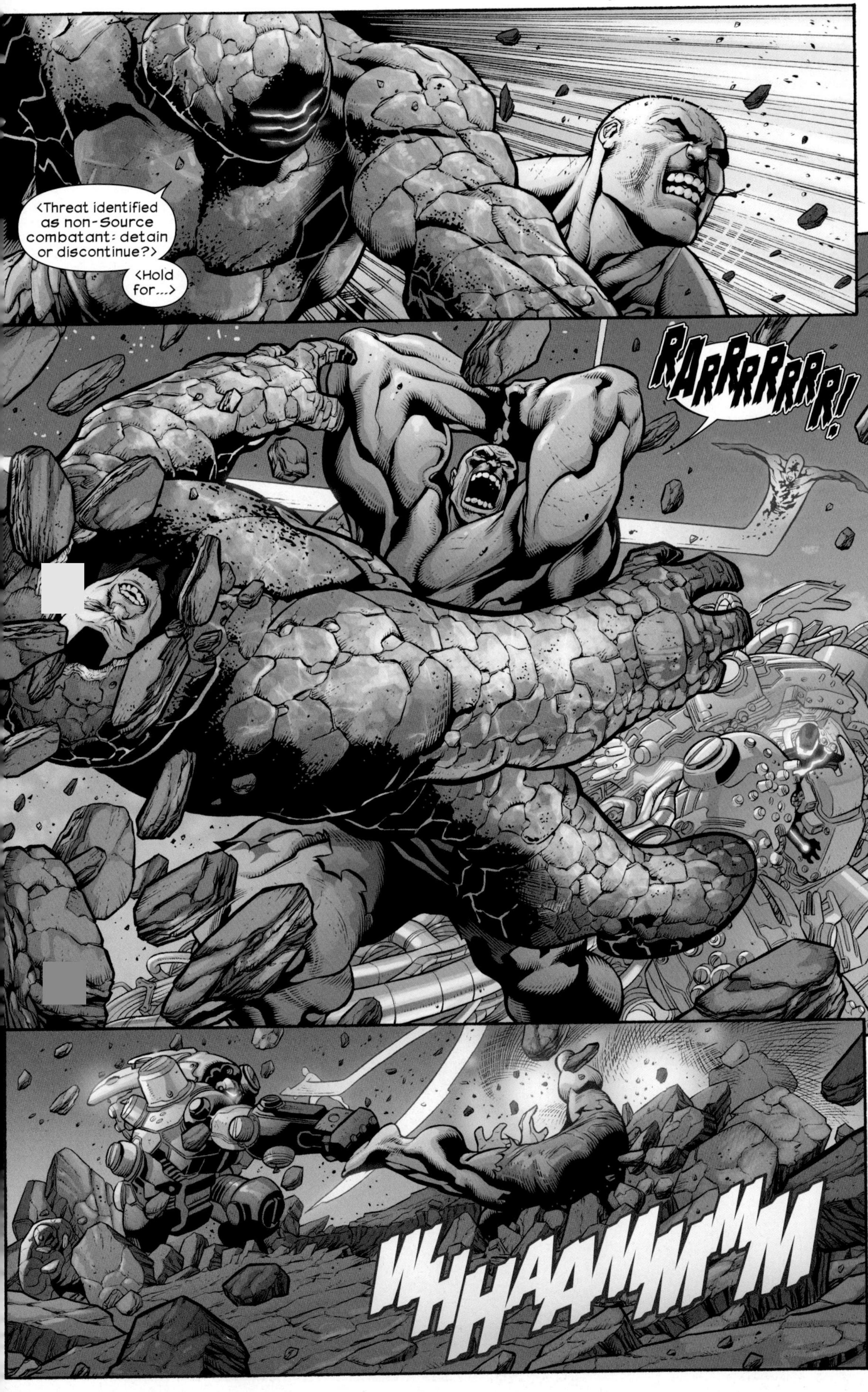
<Threat identified as non-Source combatant: detain or discontinue?>
<Hold for...>
RARRRRRRR!
WHHAAMMMM

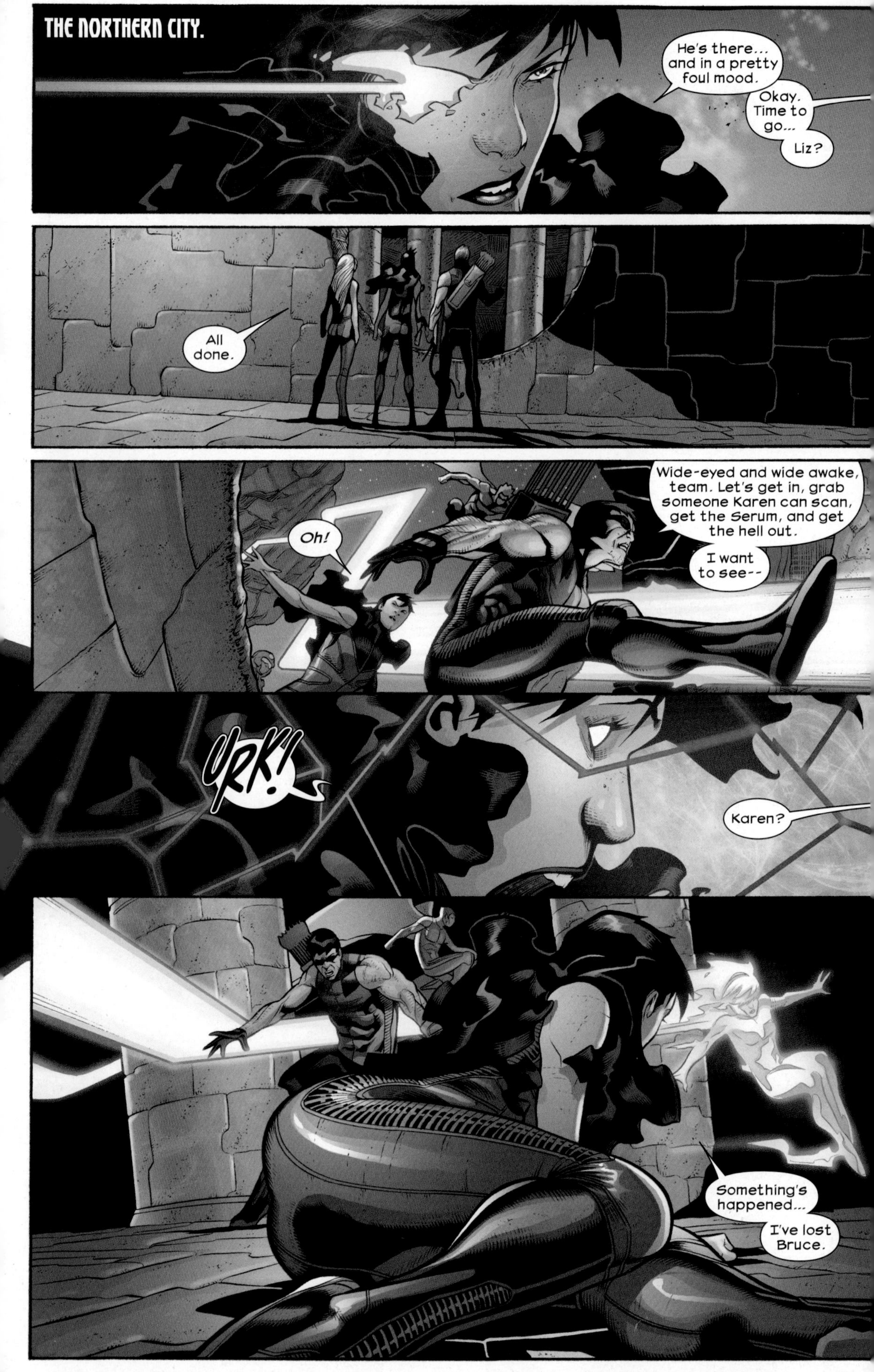
THE NORTHERN CITY.
He's there... and in a pretty foul mood.
Okay. Time to go...
Liz?
All done.
Wide-eyed and wide awake, team. Let's get in, grab someone Karen can scan, get the Serum, and get the hell out.
Oh!
I want to see--
URK!
Karen?
Something's happened...
I've lost Bruce.

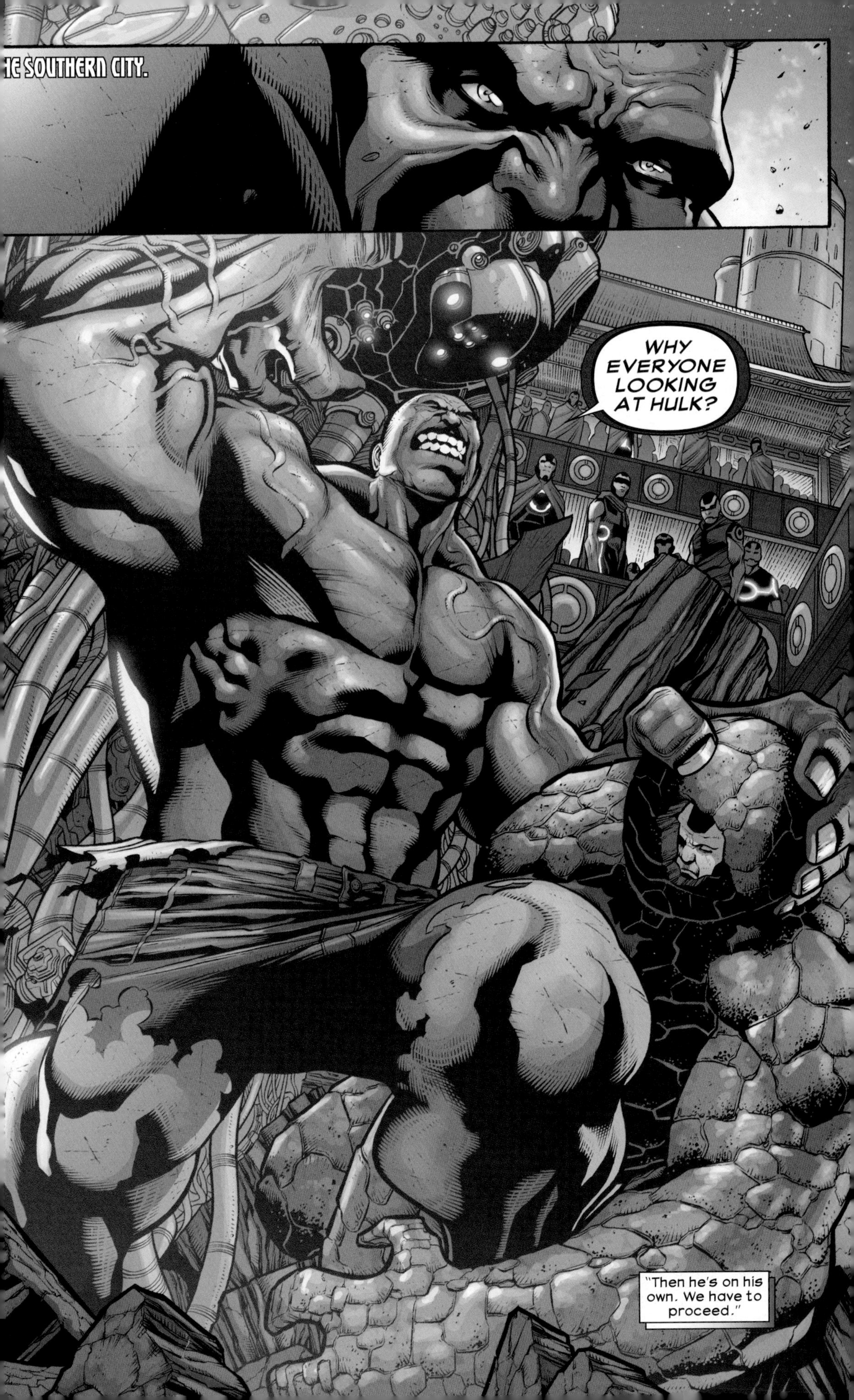

HE SOUTHERN CITY.
WHY EVERYONE LOOKING AT HULK?
"Then he's on his own. We have to proceed."

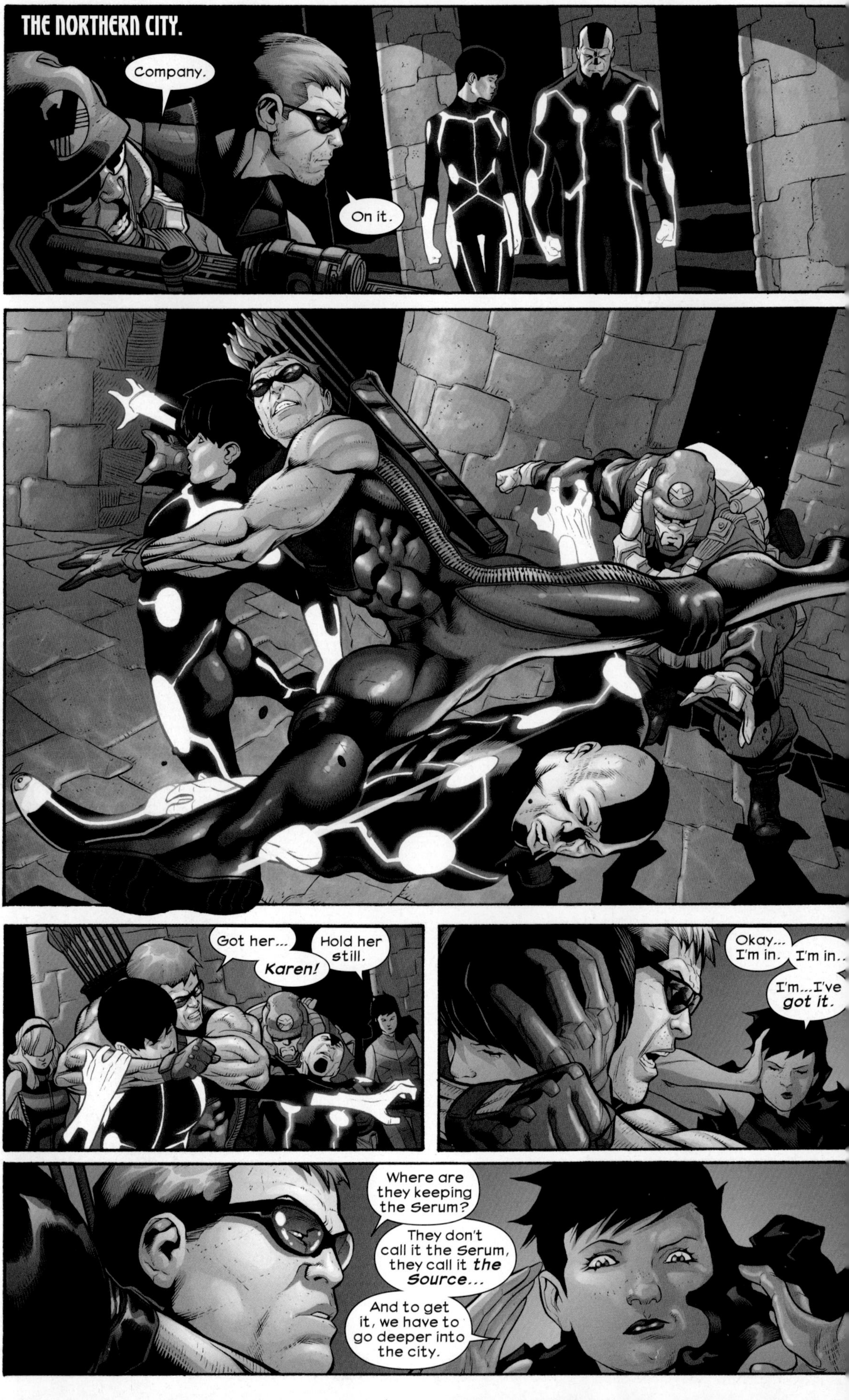
THE NORTHERN CITY.
Company.
On it.
Got her...
Karen!
Hold her still.
Okay... I'm in.
I'm in...
I'm... I've got it.
Where are they keeping the Serum?
They don't call it the Serum, they call it the Source...
And to get it, we have to go deeper into the city.

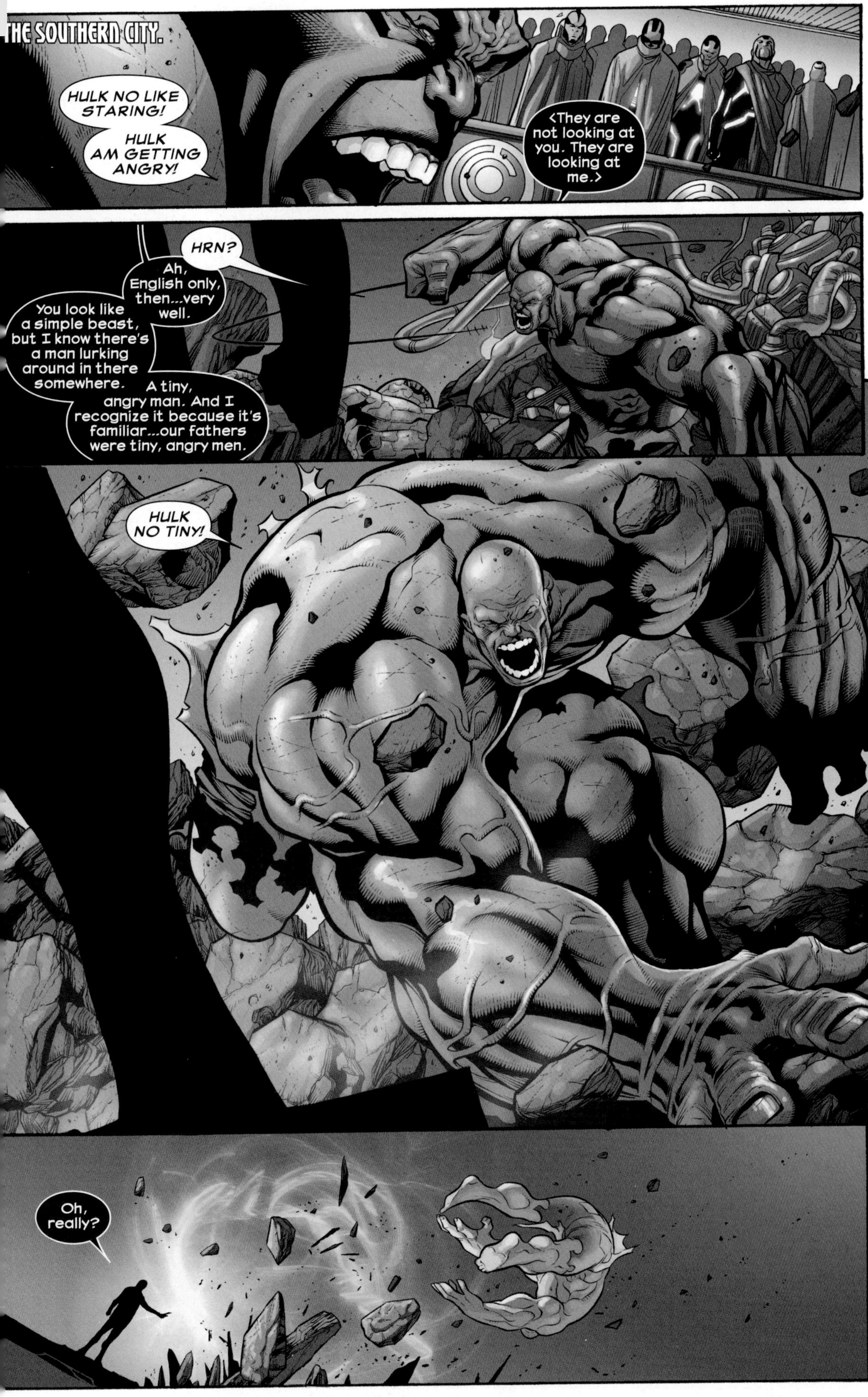
THE SOUTHERN CITY.
HULK NO LIKE STARING!
HULK AM GETTING ANGRY!
<They are not looking at you. They are looking at me.>
HRN?
Ah, English only, then...very well.
You look like a simple beast, but I know there's a man lurking around in there somewhere.
A tiny, angry man. And I recognize it because it's familiar...our fathers were tiny, angry men.
HULK NO TINY!
Oh, really?

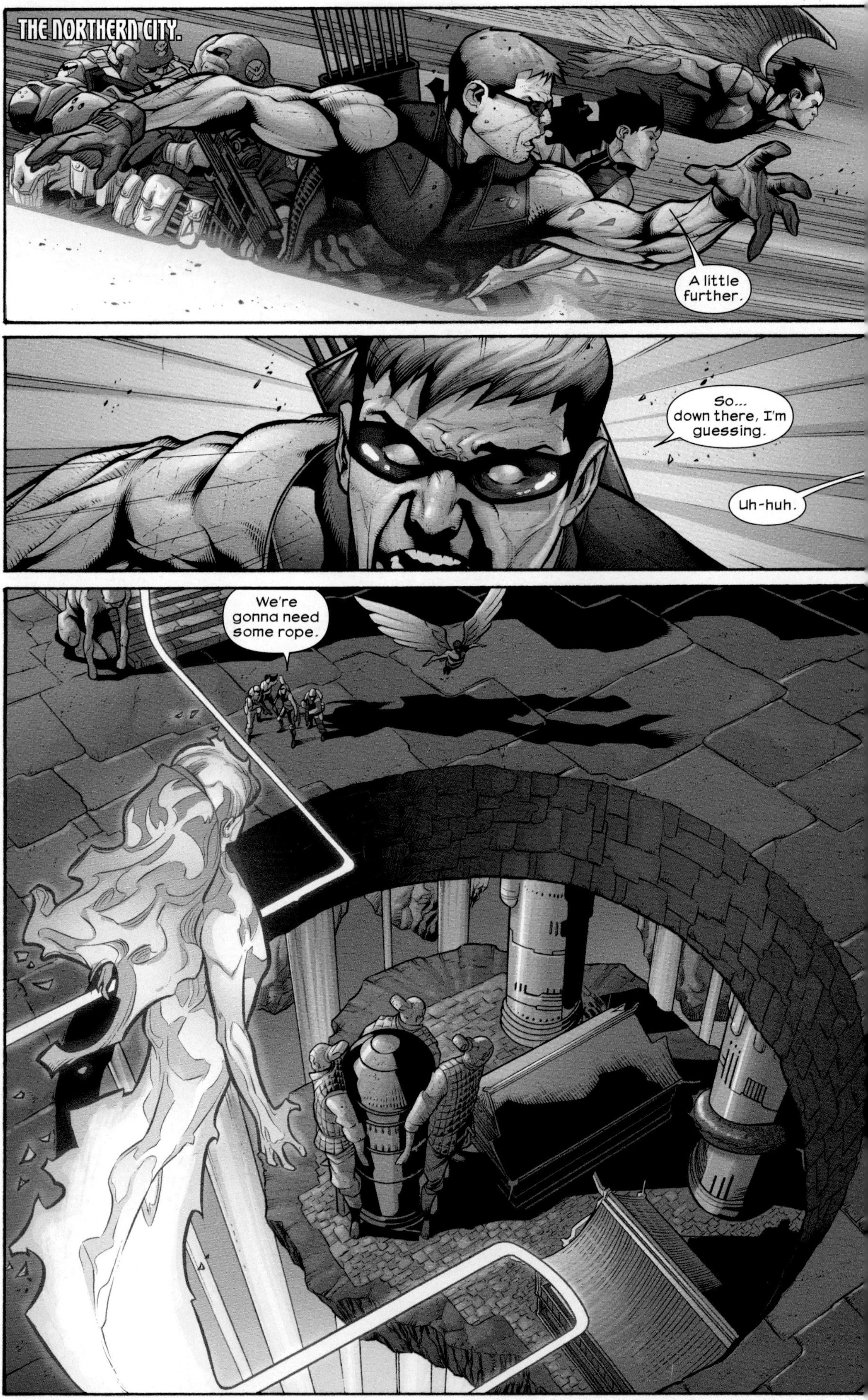
THE NORTHERN CITY.
A little further.
So... down there, I'm guessing.
Uh-huh.
We're gonna need some rope.

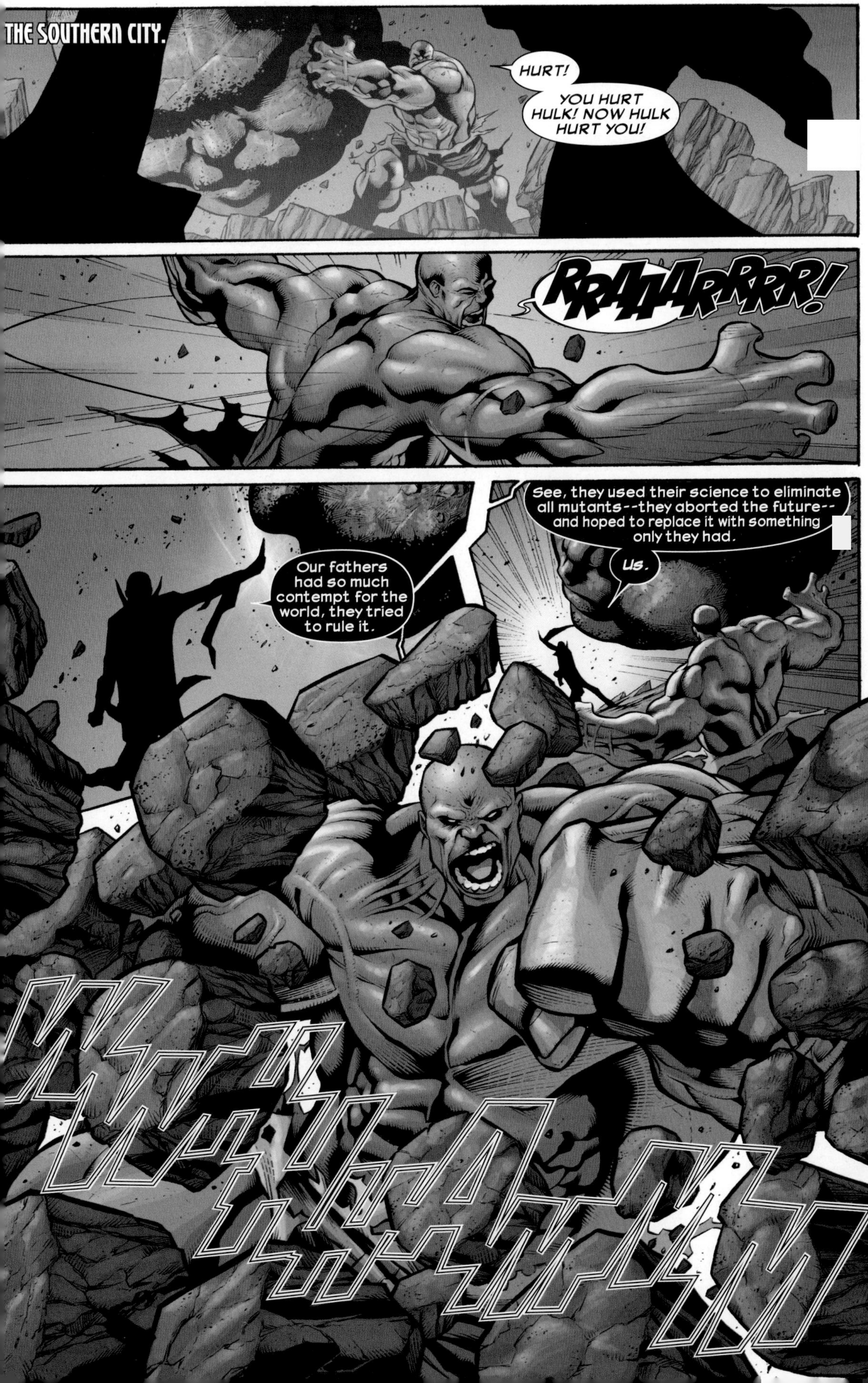
THE SOUTHERN CITY.
HURT!
YOU HURT HULK! NOW HULK HURT YOU!
RRAAARRRR!
Our fathers had so much contempt for the world, they tried to rule it.
See, they used their science to eliminate all mutants--they aborted the future--and hoped to replace it with something only they had.
Us.

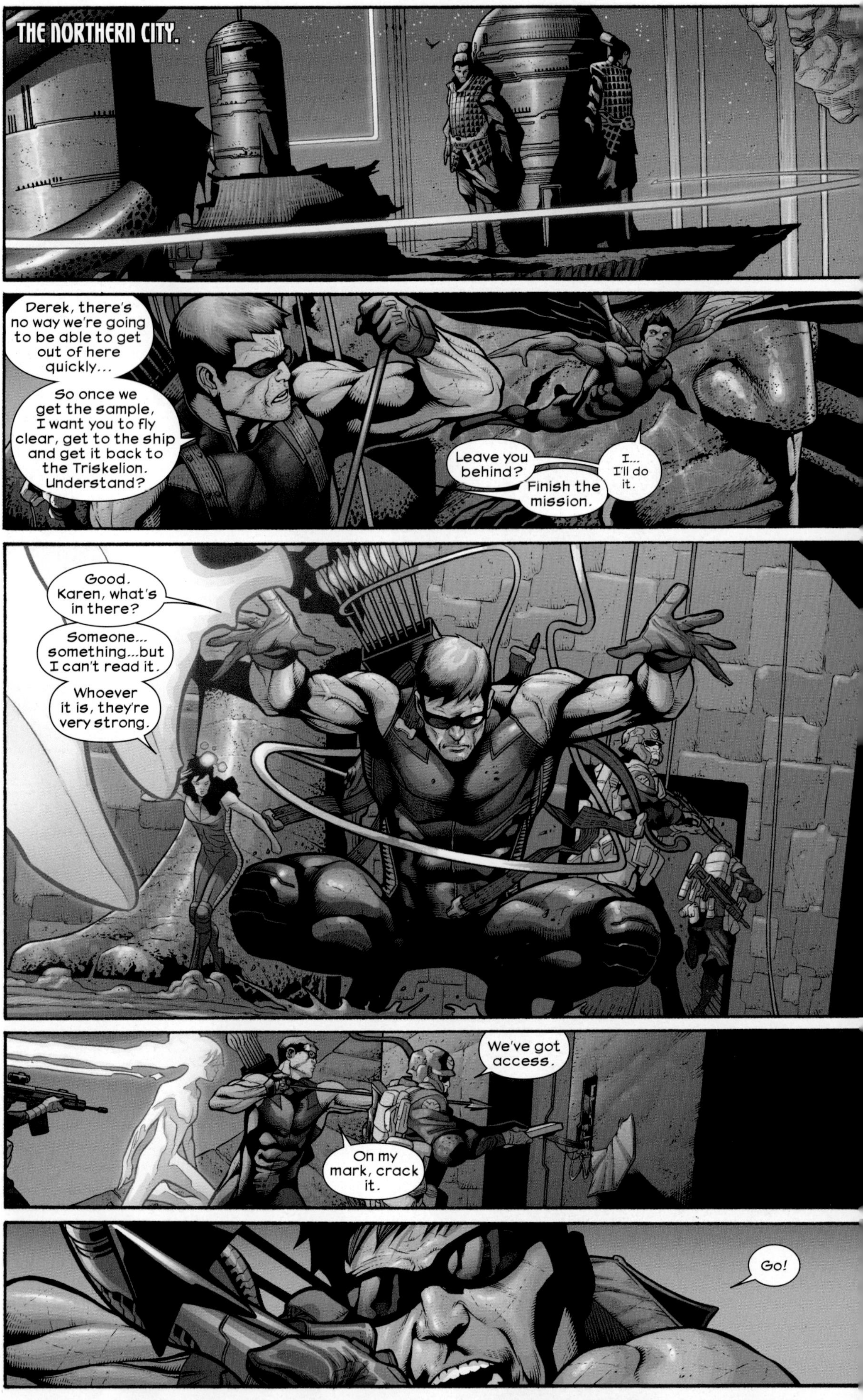
THE NORTHERN CITY.
Derek, there's no way we're going to be able to get out of here quickly...
So once we get the sample, I want you to fly clear, get to the ship and get it back to the Triskelion. Understand?
Leave you behind?
Finish the mission.
I... I'll do it.
Good. Karen, what's in there?
Someone... something...but I can't read it.
Whoever it is, they're very strong.
We've got access.
On my mark, crack it.
Go!

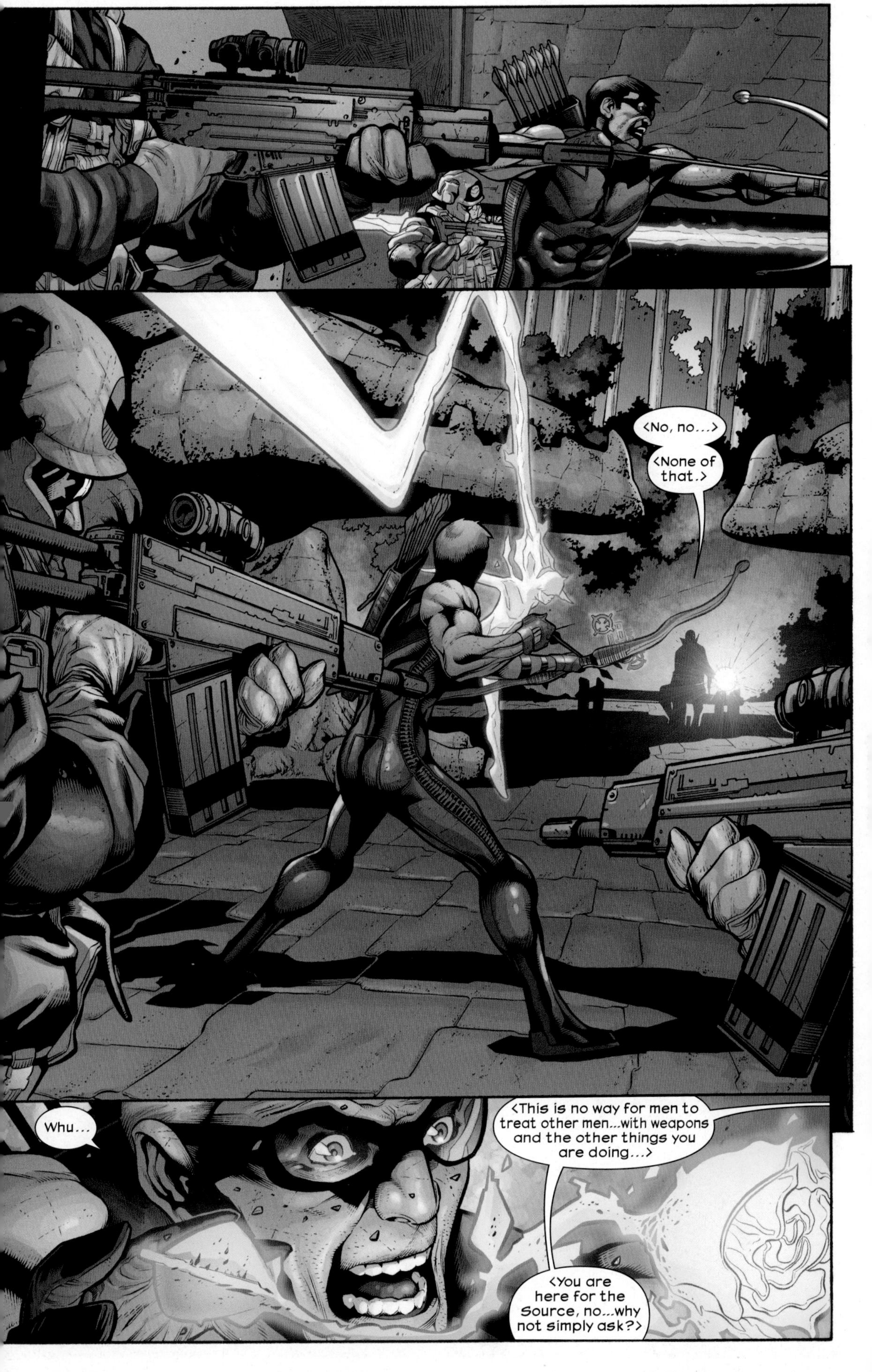
<No, no...>
<None of that.>
Whu...
<This is no way for men to treat other men...with weapons and the other things you are doing...>
<You are here for the Source, no...why not simply ask?>

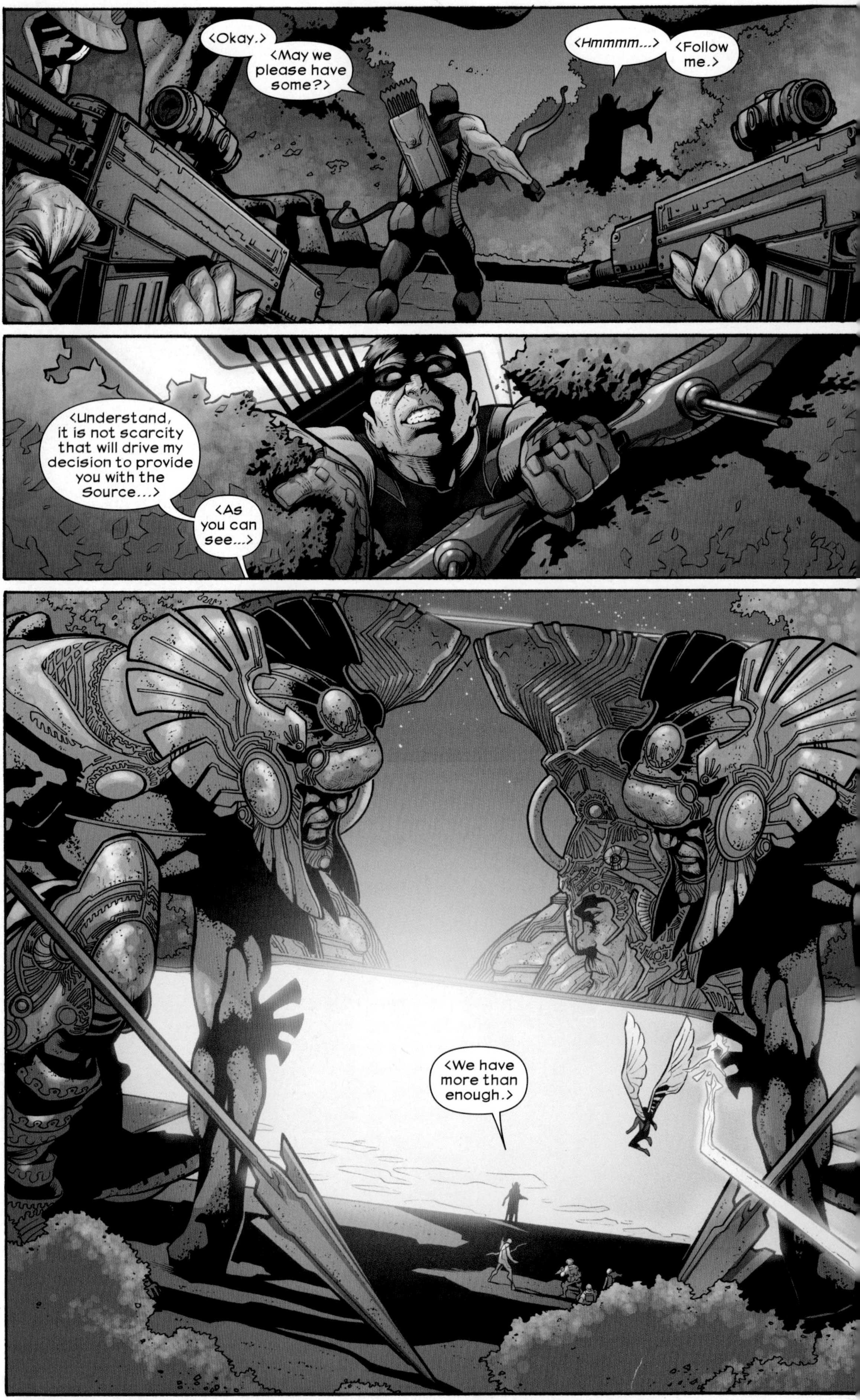
<Okay.>
<May we please have some?>
<Hmmmm...>
<Follow me.>
<Understand, it is not scarcity that will drive my decision to provide you with the Source...>
<As you can see...>
<We have more than enough.>

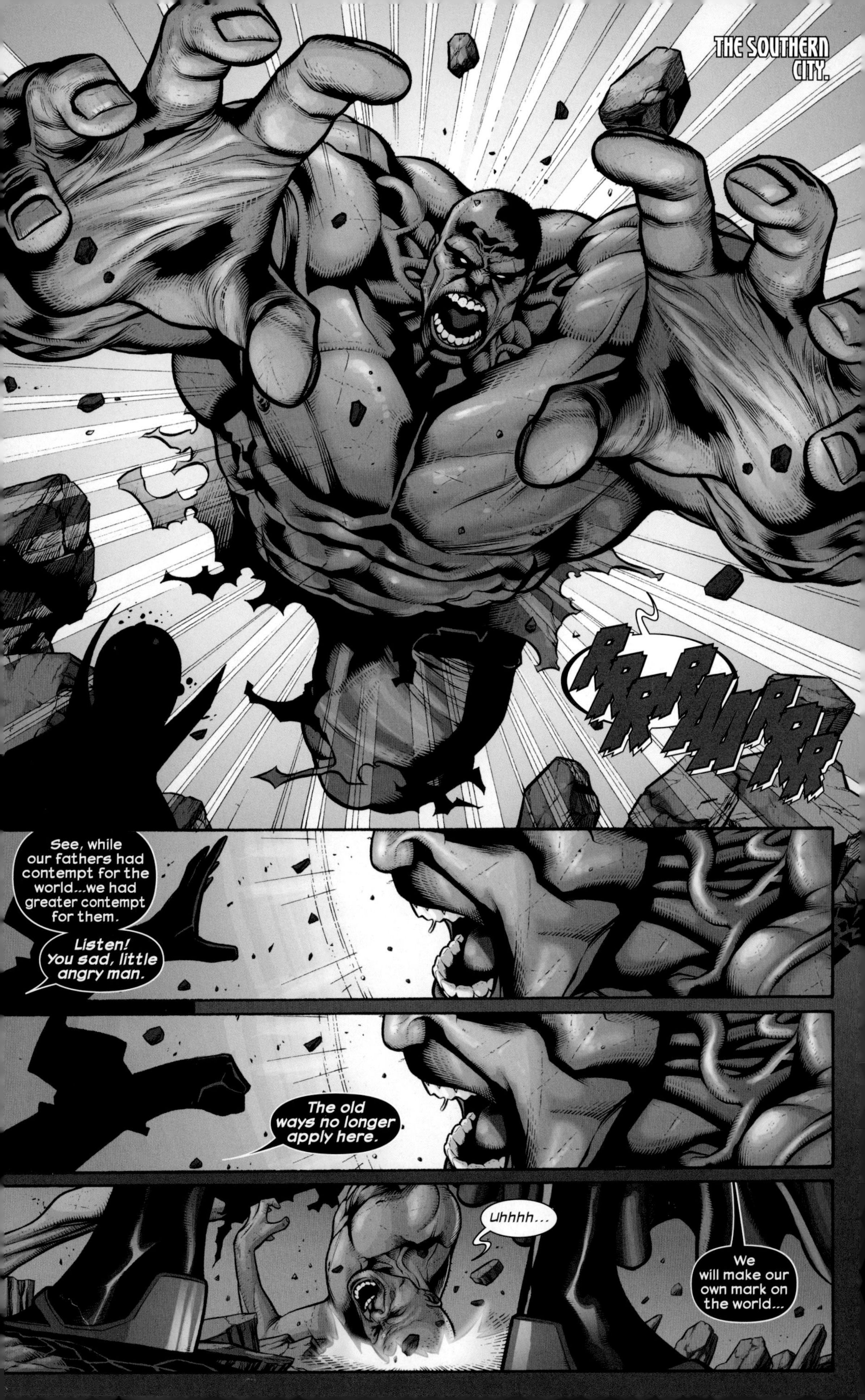
THE SOUTHERN CITY.
See, while our fathers had contempt for the world...we had greater contempt for them.
Listen! You sad, little angry man.
The old ways no longer apply here.
Uhhhh...
We will make our own mark on the world...

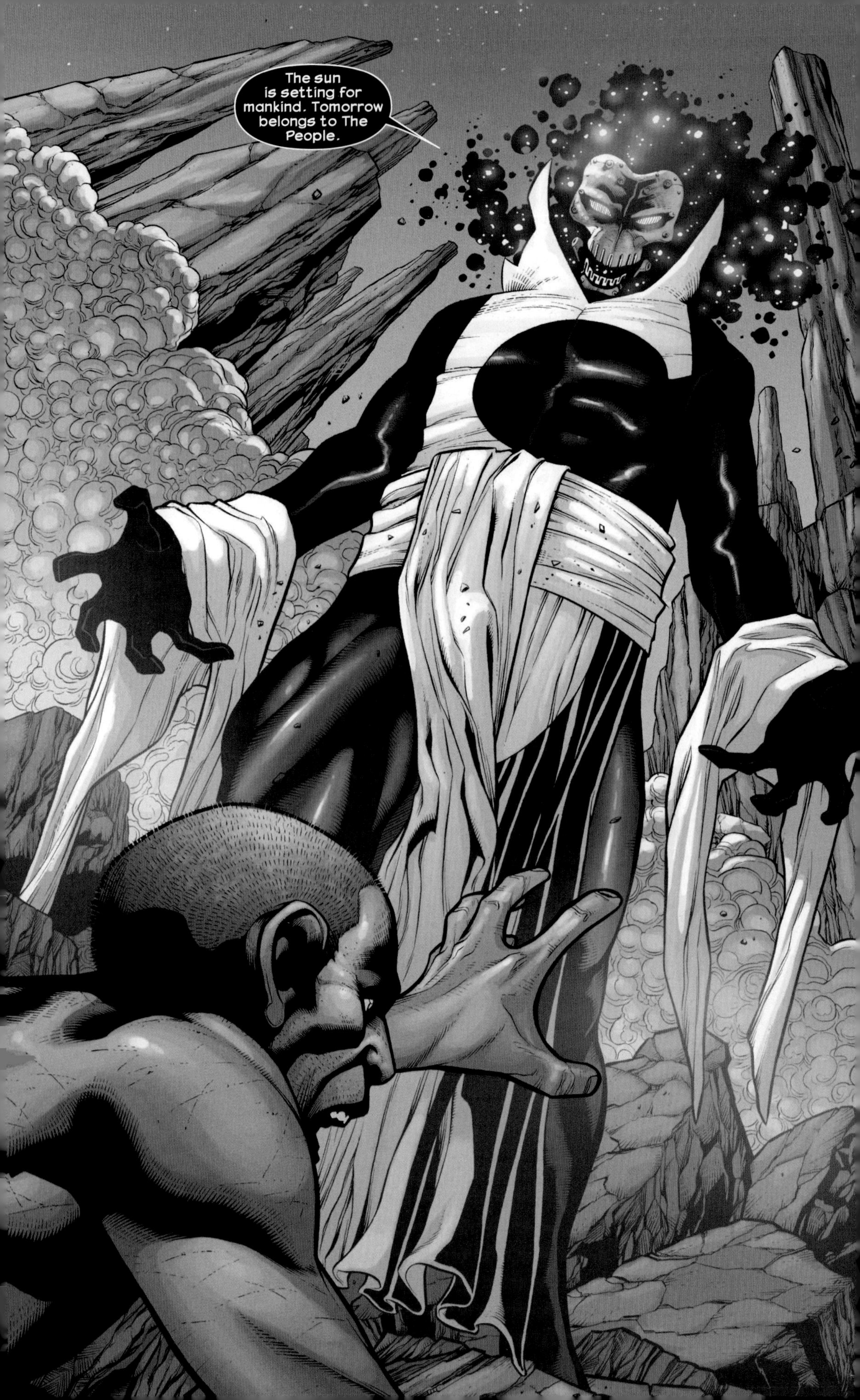
The sun is setting for mankind. Tomorrow belongs to The People.

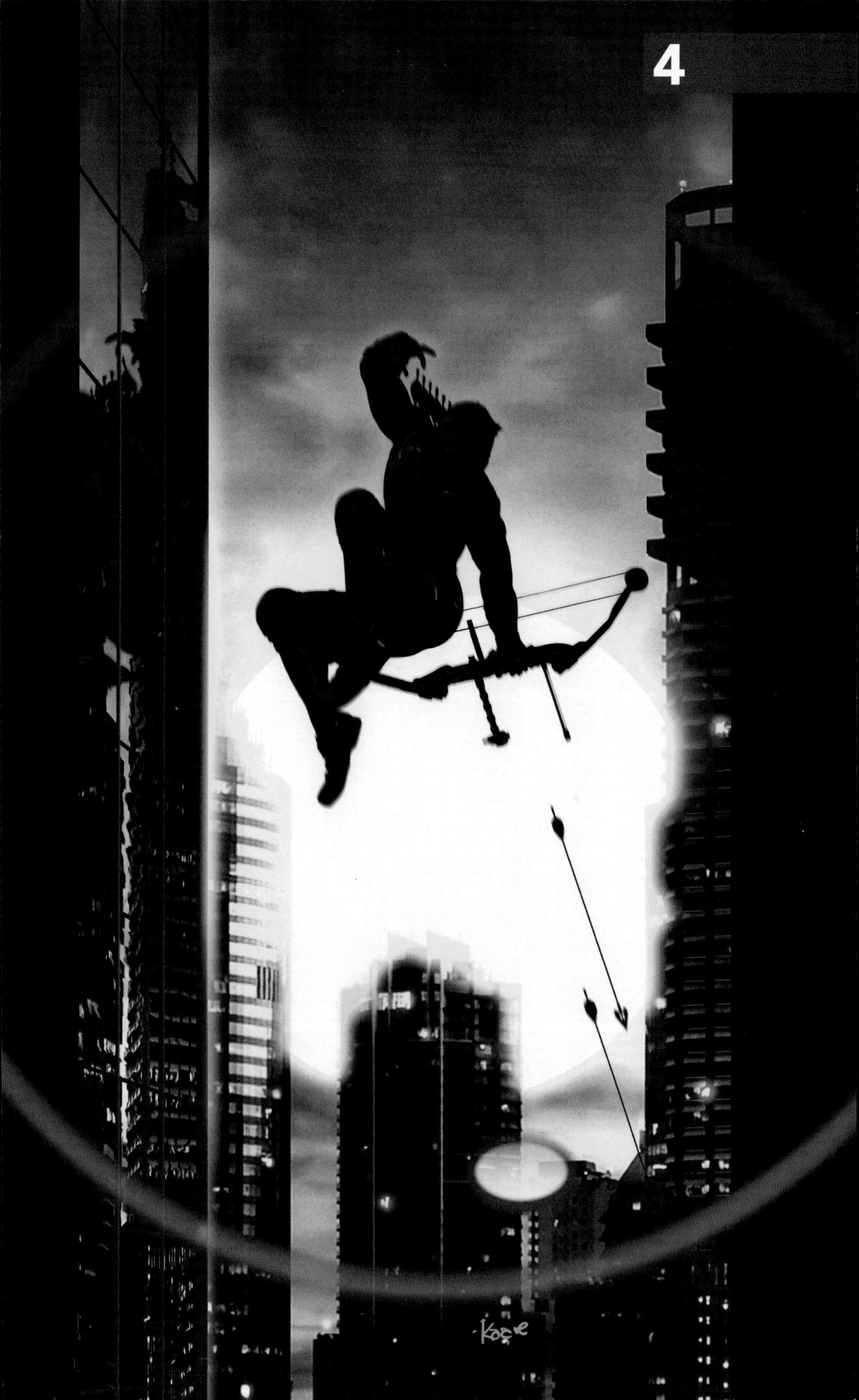
4

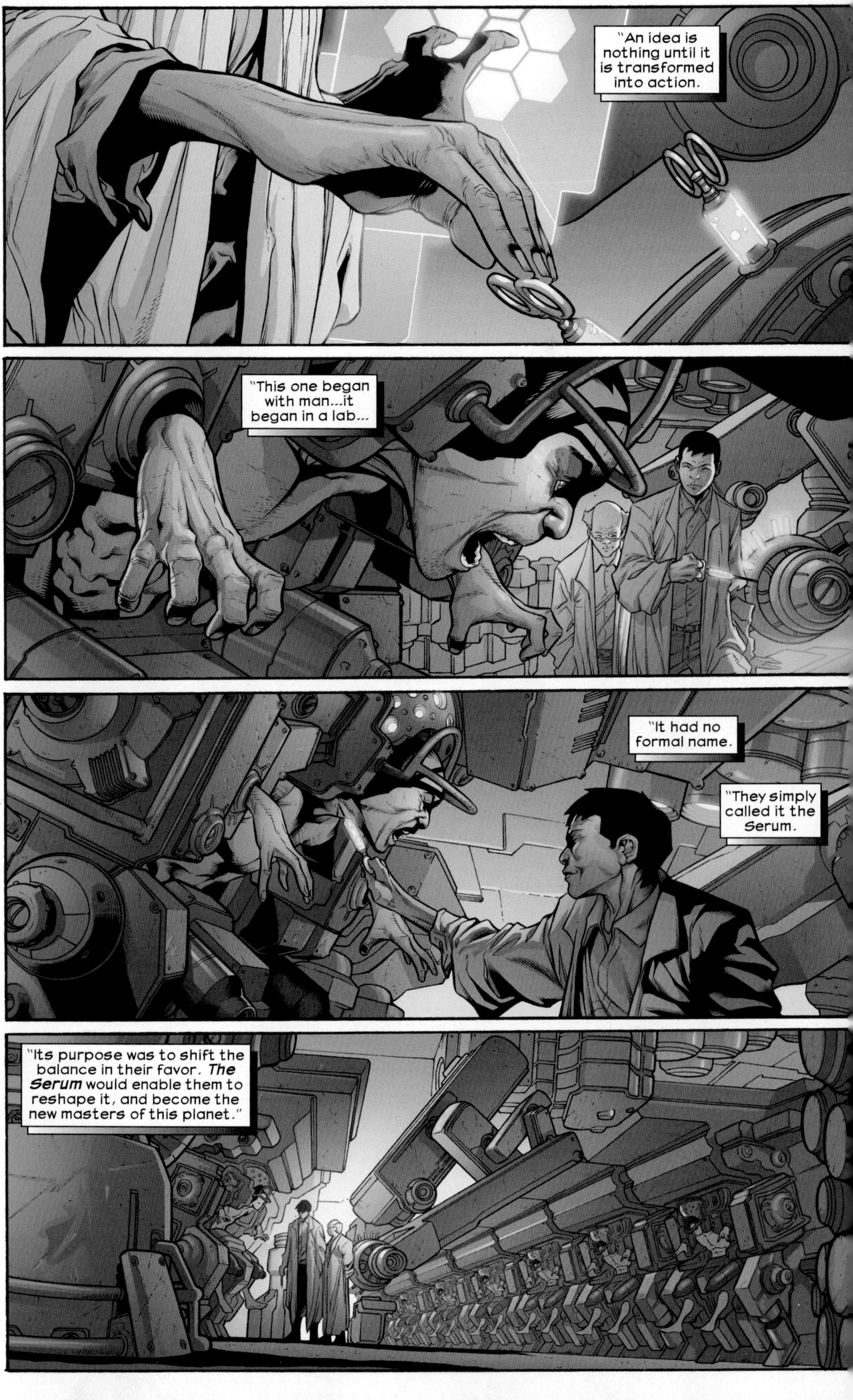
"An idea is nothing until it is transformed into action.
"This one began with man...it began in a lab...
"It had no formal name.
"They simply called it the *Serum*.
"Its purpose was to shift the balance in their favor. ***The Serum*** would enable them to reshape it, and become the new masters of this planet."

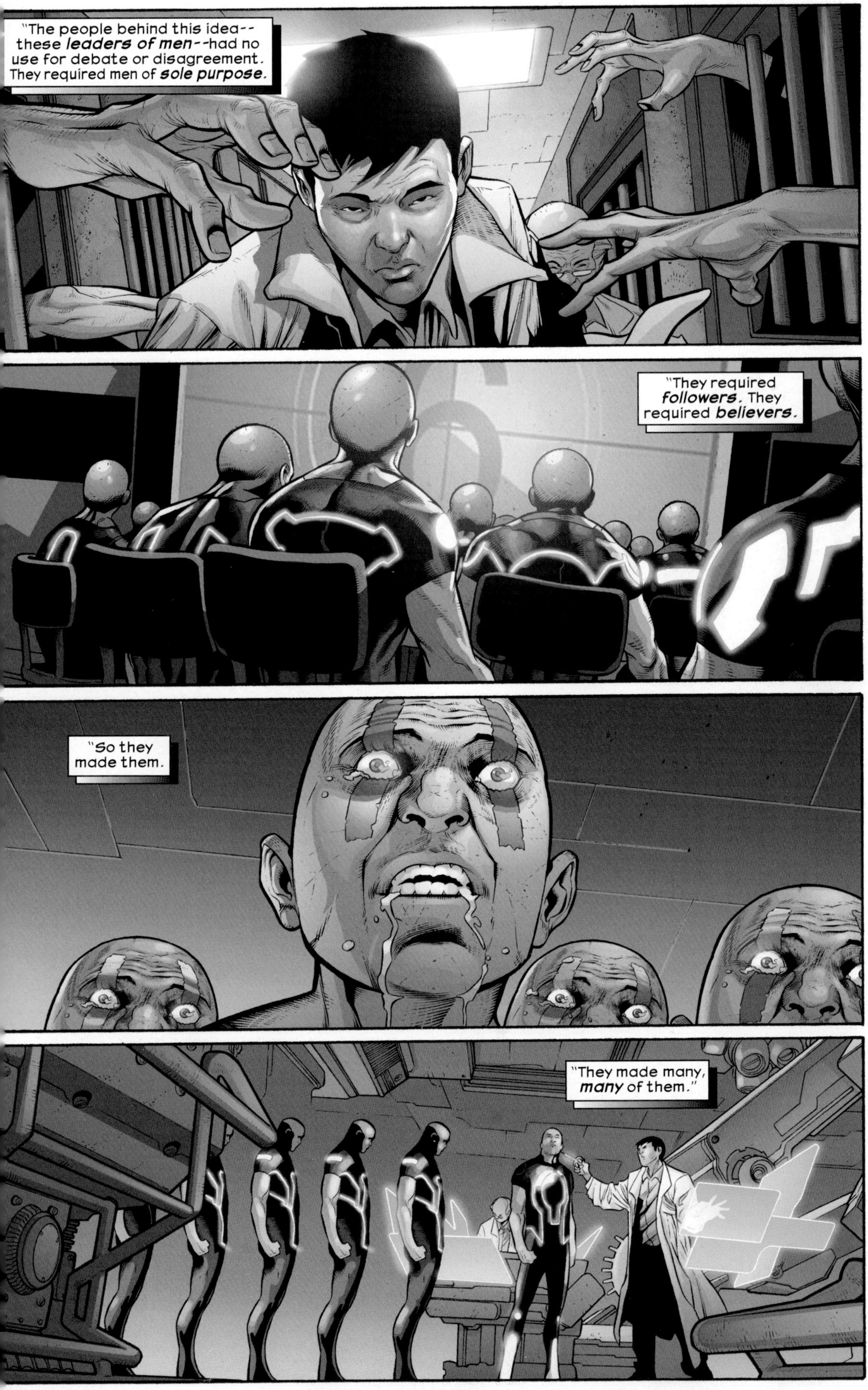
"The people behind this idea--these *leaders of men*--had no use for debate or disagreement. They required men of *sole purpose*.
"They required *followers*. They required *believers*.
"So they made them.
"They made many, *many* of them."

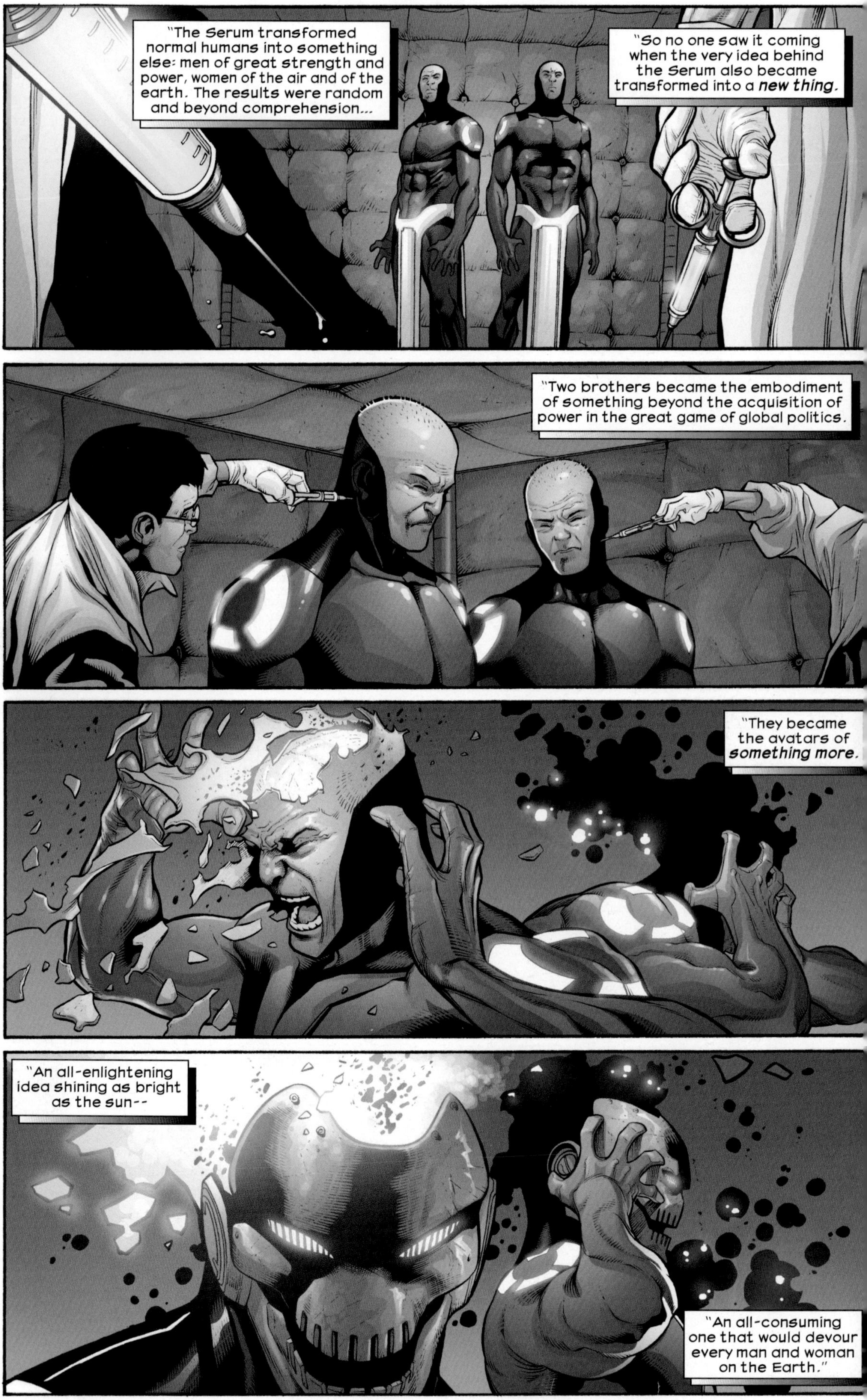
"The Serum transformed normal humans into something else: men of great strength and power, women of the air and of the earth. The results were random and beyond comprehension...
"So no one saw it coming when the very idea behind the Serum also became transformed into a *new thing.*
"Two brothers became the embodiment of something beyond the acquisition of power in the great game of global politics.
"They became the avatars of *something more.*
"An all-enlightening idea shining as bright as the sun--
"An all-consuming one that would devour every man and woman on the Earth."

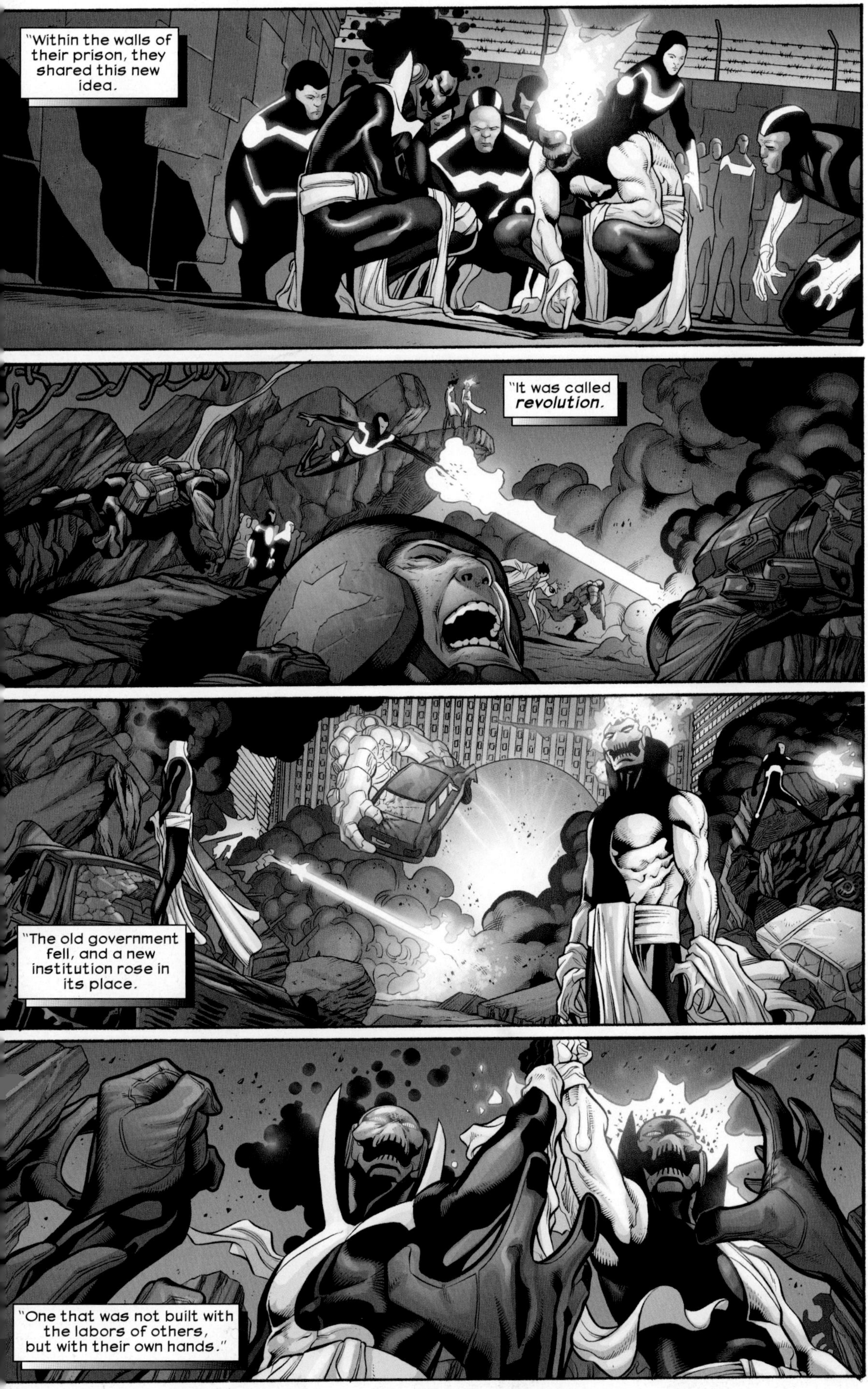
"Within the walls of their prison, they shared this new idea.
"It was called *revolution*.
"The old government fell, and a new institution rose in its place.
"One that was not built with the labors of others, but with their own hands."

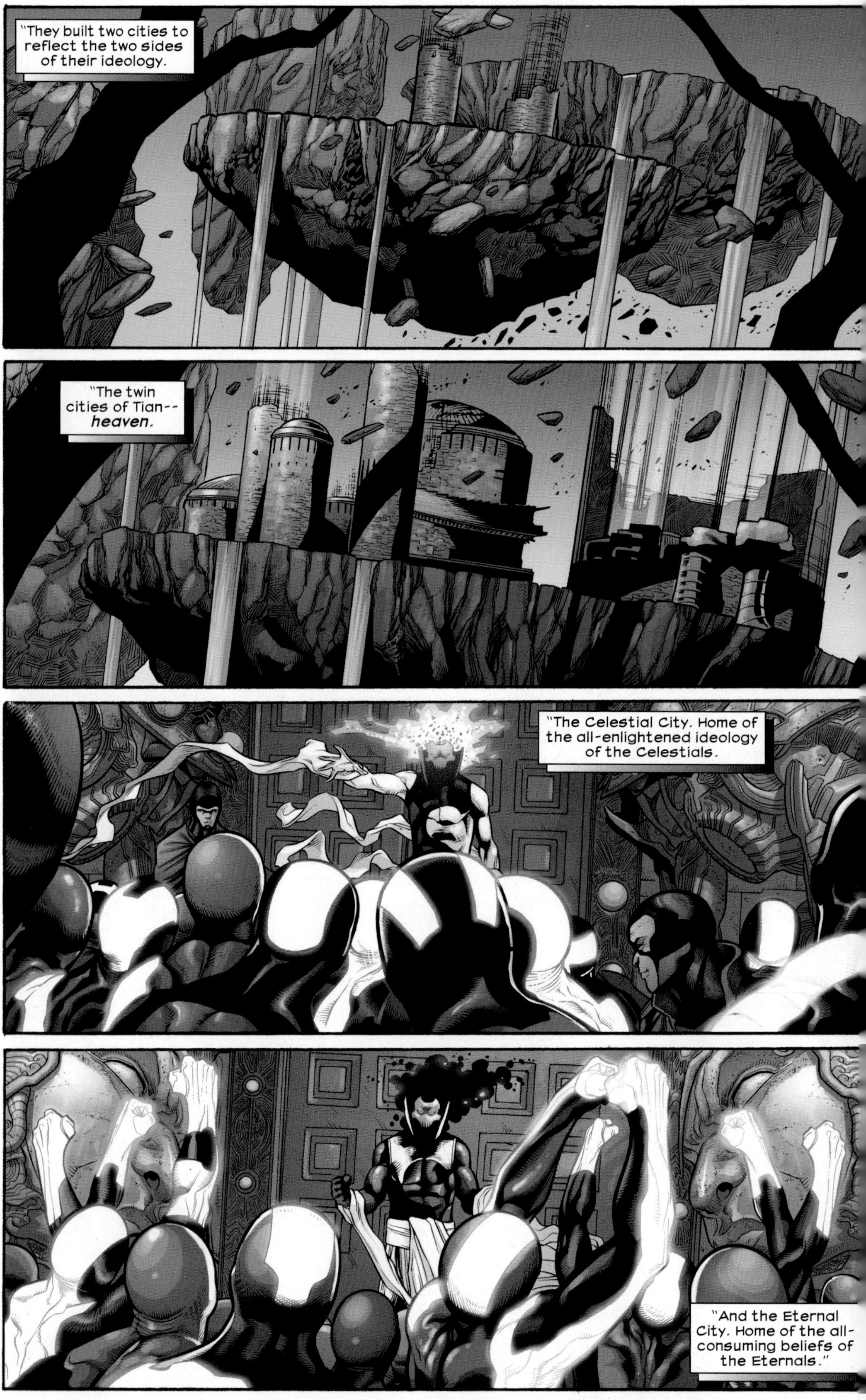
"They built two cities to reflect the two sides of their ideology.
"The twin cities of Tian--*heaven.*
"The Celestial City. Home of the all-enlightened ideology of the Celestials.
"And the Eternal City. Home of the all-consuming beliefs of the Eternals."

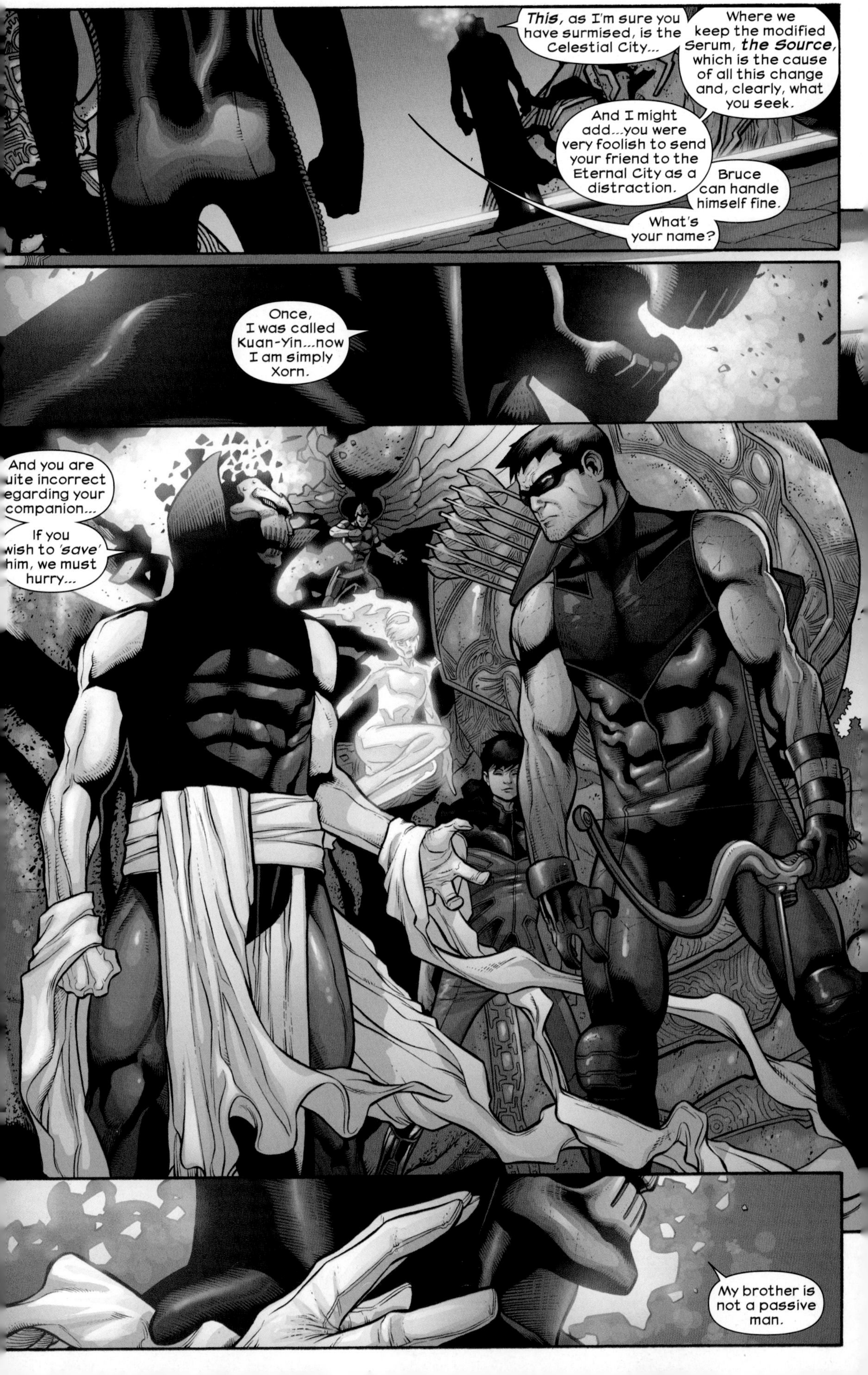
This, as I'm sure you have surmised, is the Celestial City...
Where we keep the modified Serum, the Source, which is the cause of all this change and, clearly, what you seek.
And I might add...you were very foolish to send your friend to the Eternal City as a distraction.
Bruce can handle himself fine.
What's your name?
Once, I was called Kuan-Yin...now I am simply Xorn.
And you are uite incorrect egarding your companion...
If you wish to 'save' him, we must hurry...
My brother is not a passive man.

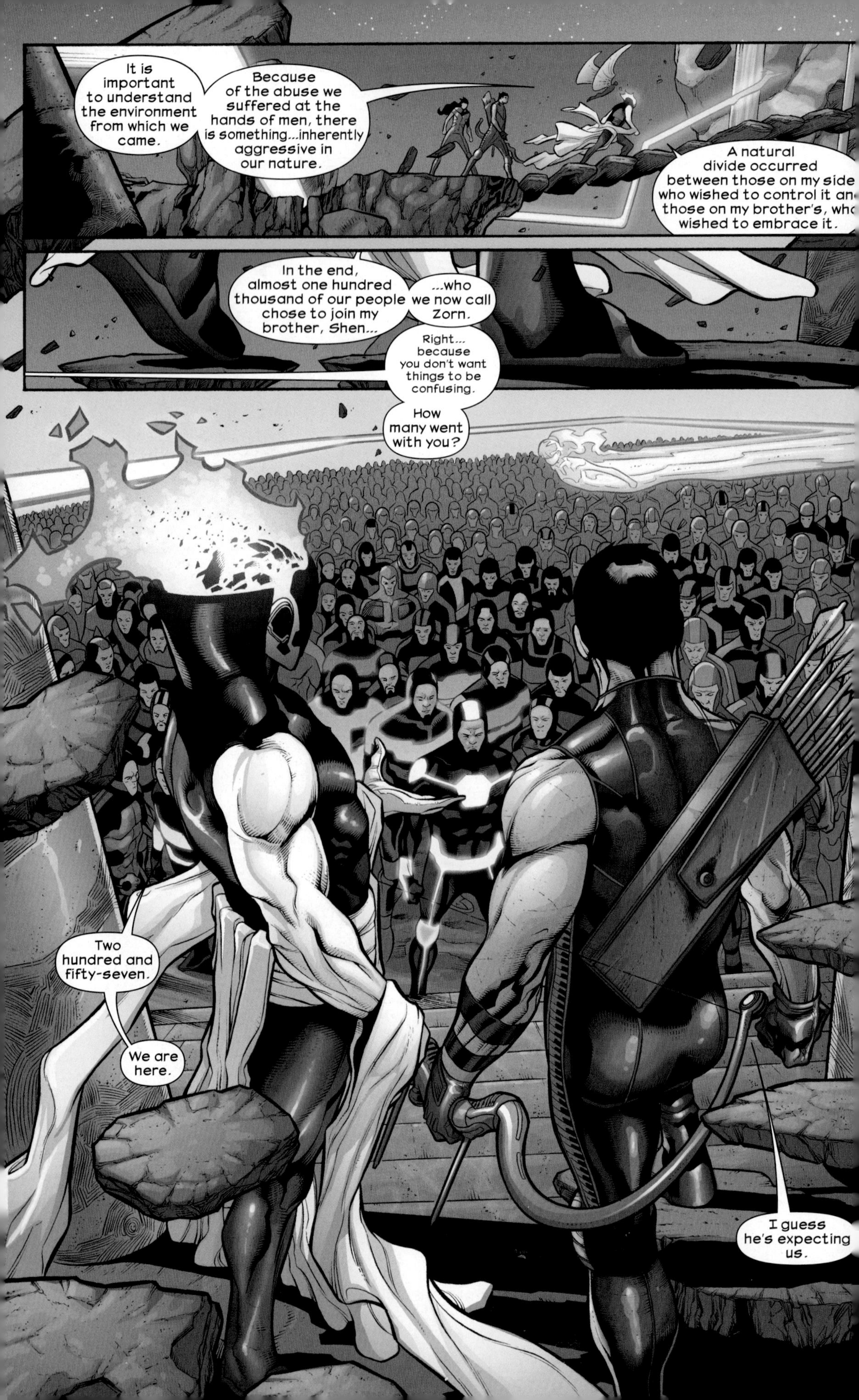
It is important to understand the environment from which we came.
Because of the abuse we suffered at the hands of men, there is something...inherently aggressive in our nature.
A natural divide occurred between those on my side who wished to control it an those on my brother's, wh wished to embrace it.
In the end, almost one hundred thousand of our people chose to join my brother, Shen...
...who we now call Zorn.
Right... because you don't want things to be confusing.
How many went with you?
Two hundred and fifty-seven.
We are here.
I guess he's expecting us.

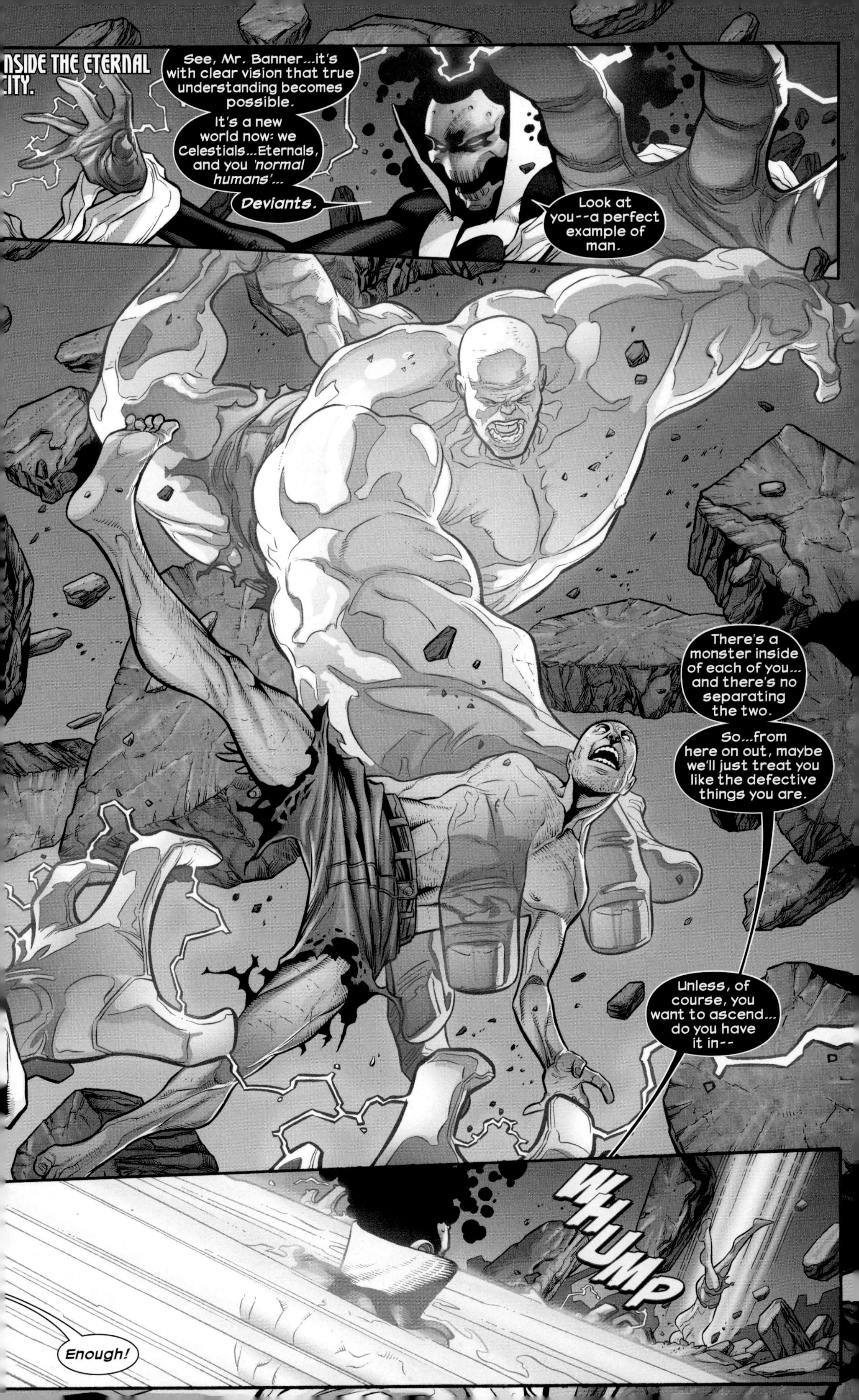
NSIDE THE ETERNAL CITY.
See, Mr. Banner...it's with clear vision that true understanding becomes possible.
It's a new world now: we Celestials...Eternals, and you 'normal humans'...
Deviants.
Look at you--a perfect example of man.
There's a monster inside of each of you... and there's no separating the two.
So...from here on out, maybe we'll just treat you like the defective things you are.
Unless, of course, you want to ascend... do you have it in--
WHUMP
Enough!

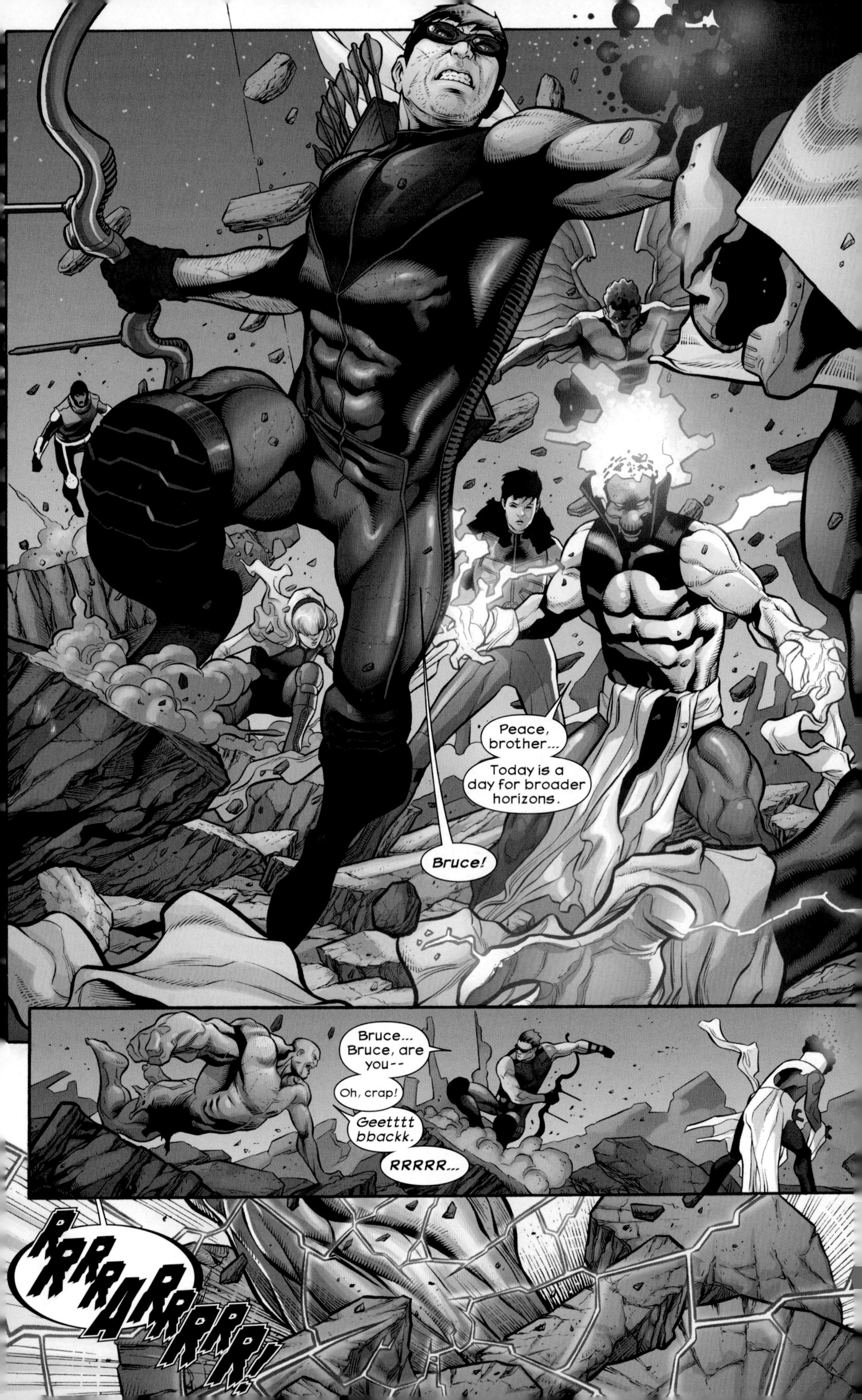
Peace, brother...
Today is a day for broader horizons.
Bruce!
Bruce... Bruce, are you--
Oh, crap!
Geetttt bbackk.
RRRRR...
RRRRARRRRR!

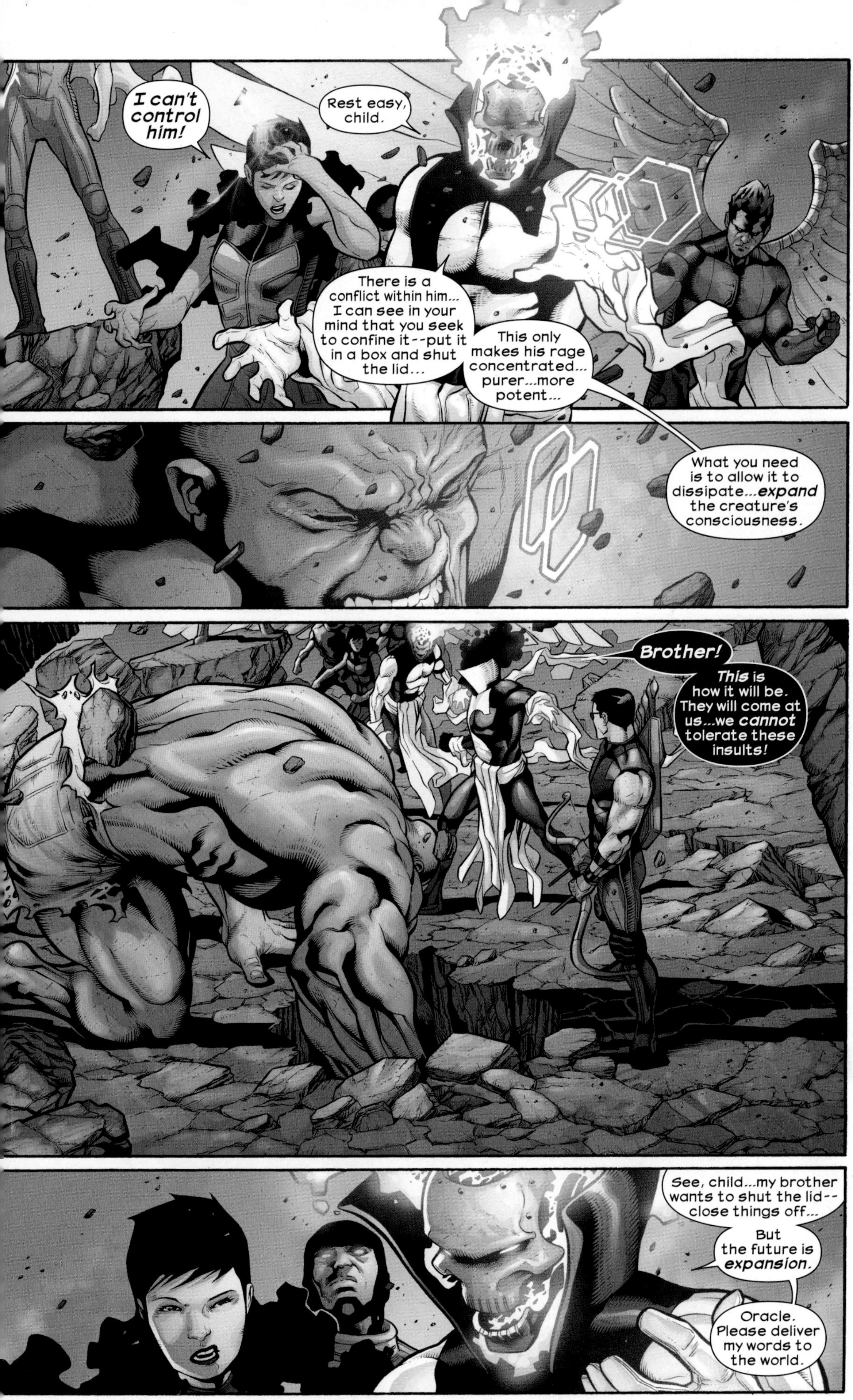
I can't control him!
Rest easy, child.
There is a conflict within him... I can see in your mind that you seek to confine it--put it in a box and shut the lid...
This only makes his rage concentrated... purer...more potent...
What you need is to allow it to dissipate...*expand* the creature's consciousness.
Brother!
This is how it will be. They will come at us...we *cannot* tolerate these insults!
See, child...my brother wants to shut the lid--close things off...
But the future is *expansion*.
Oracle. Please deliver my words to the world.

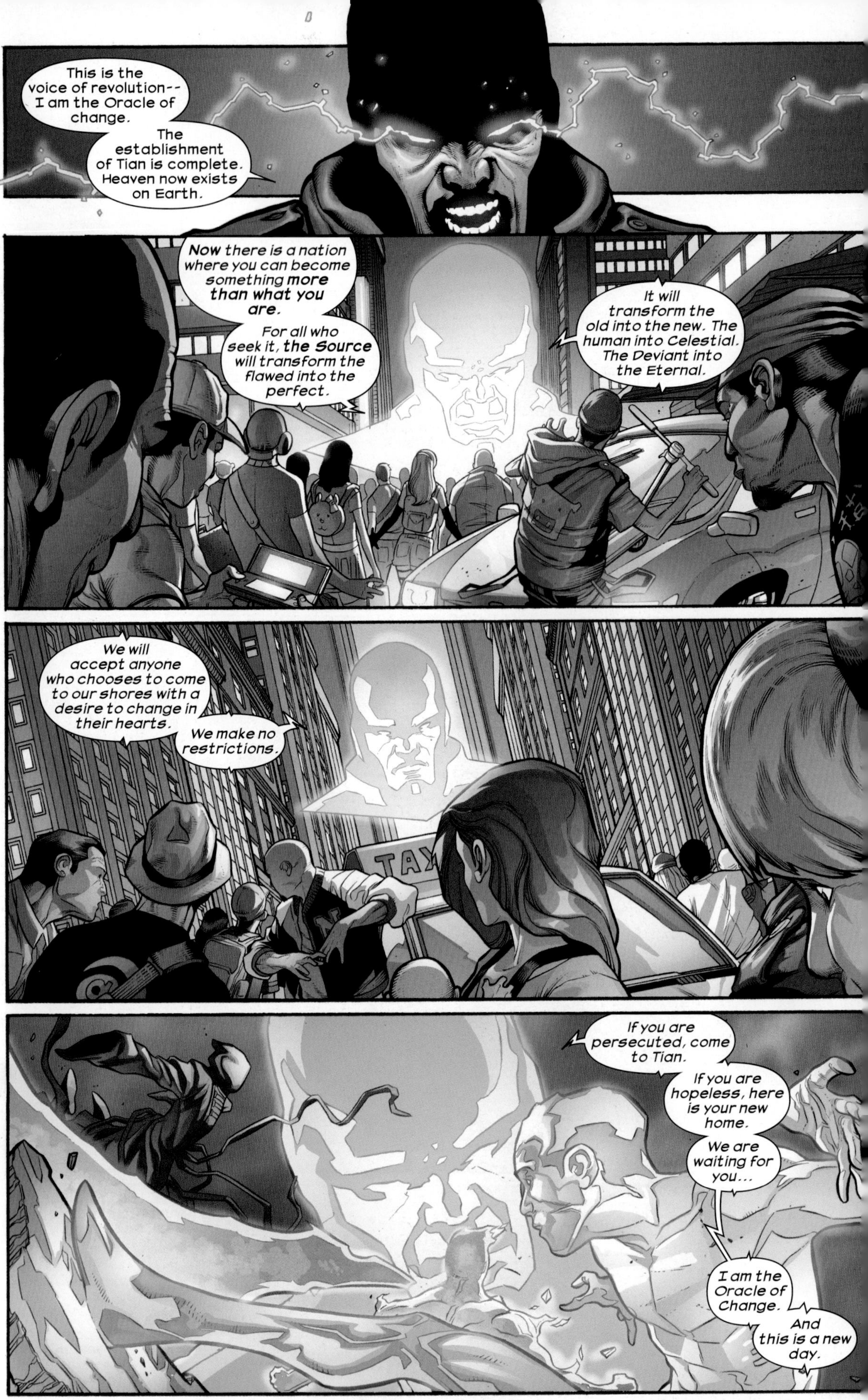
This is the voice of revolution-- I am the Oracle of change.
The establishment of Tian is complete. Heaven now exists on Earth.
Now there is a nation where you can become something more than what you are.
For all who seek it, the Source will transform the flawed into the perfect.
It will transform the old into the new. The human into Celestial. The Deviant into the Eternal.
We will accept anyone who chooses to come to our shores with a desire to change in their hearts.
We make no restrictions.
TAX
If you are persecuted, come to Tian.
If you are hopeless, here is your new home.
We are waiting for you...
I am the Oracle of Change.
And this is a new day.

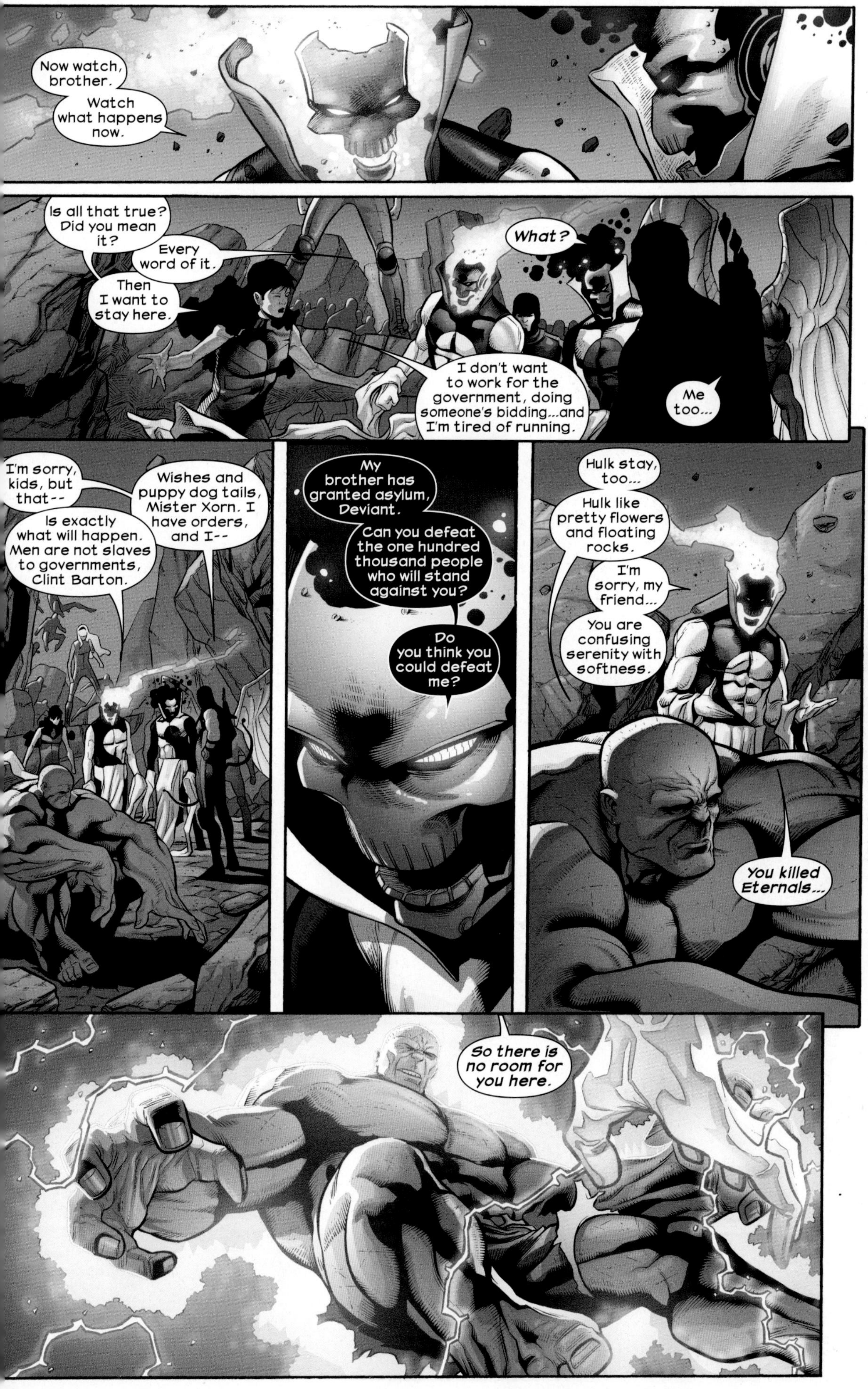
Now watch, brother.
Watch what happens now.
Is all that true? Did you mean it?
Every word of it.
Then I want to stay here.
What?
I don't want to work for the government, doing someone's bidding...and I'm tired of running.
Me too...
I'm sorry, kids, but that--
Wishes and puppy dog tails, Mister Xorn. I have orders, and I--
Is exactly what will happen. Men are not slaves to governments, Clint Barton.
My brother has granted asylum, Deviant.
Can you defeat the one hundred thousand people who will stand against you?
Do you think you could defeat me?
Hulk stay, too...
Hulk like pretty flowers and floating rocks.
I'm sorry, my friend...
You are confusing serenity with softness.
You killed Eternals...
So there is no room for you here.

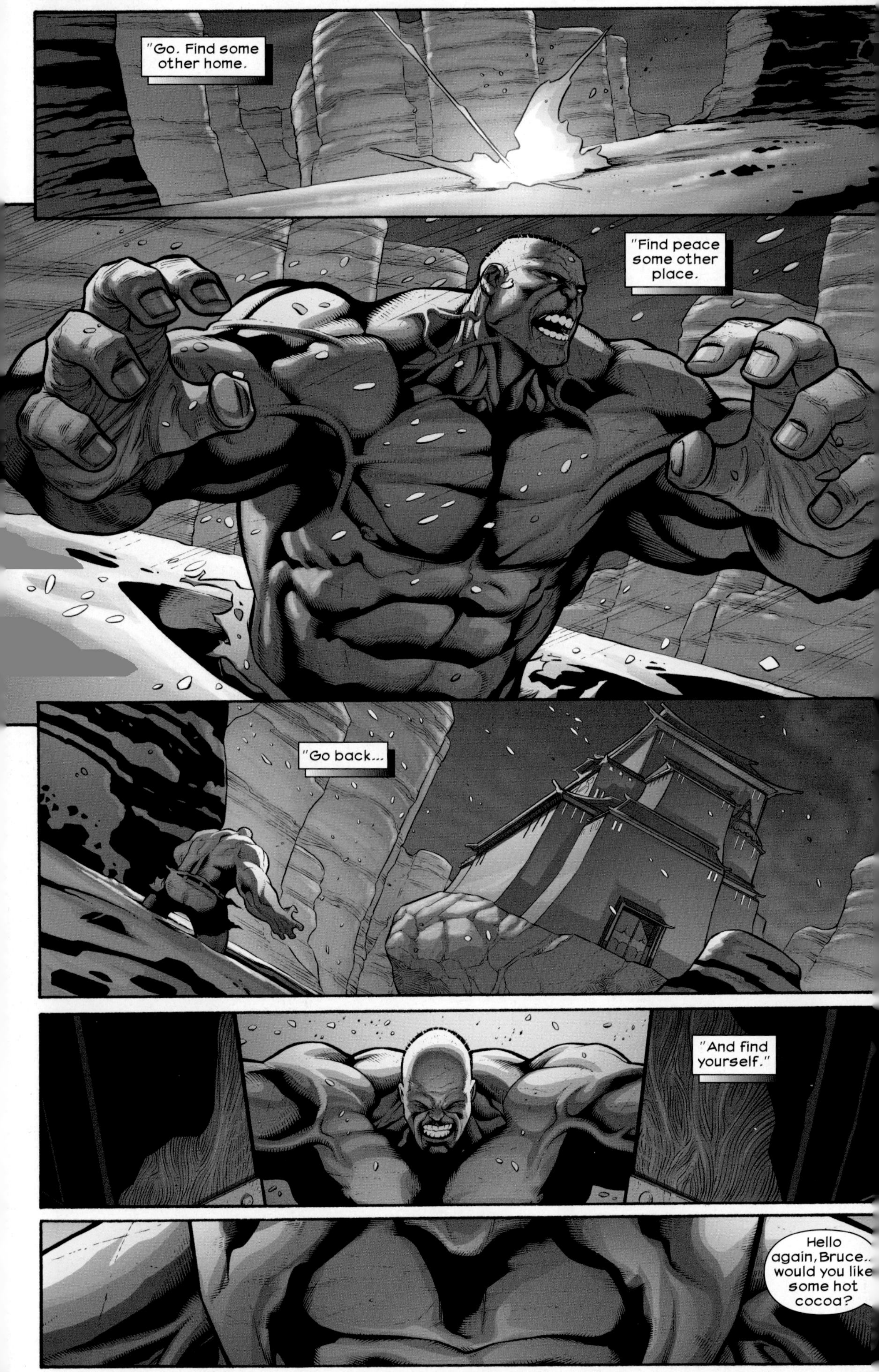
"Go. Find some other home.
"Find peace some other place.
"Go back...
"And find yourself."
Hello again, Bruce... would you like some hot cocoa?

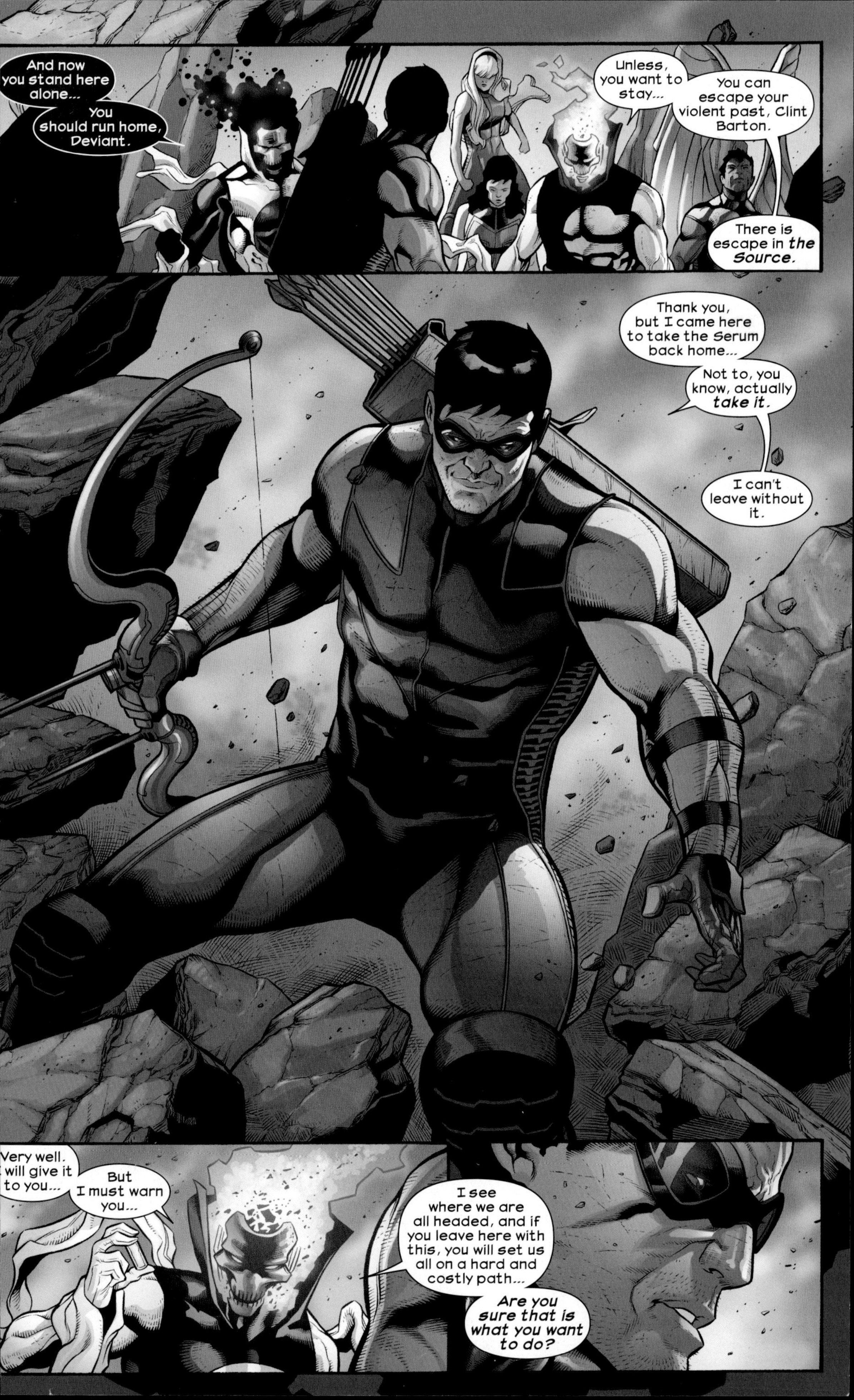
And now you stand here alone...
You should run home, Deviant.
Unless, you want to stay...
You can escape your violent past, Clint Barton.
There is escape in *the Source.*
Thank you, but I came here to take the Serum back home...
Not to, you know, actually *take it.*
I can't leave without it.
Very well. will give it to you...
But I must warn you...
I see where we are all headed, and if you leave here with this, you will set us all on a hard and costly path...
Are you sure that is what you want to do?

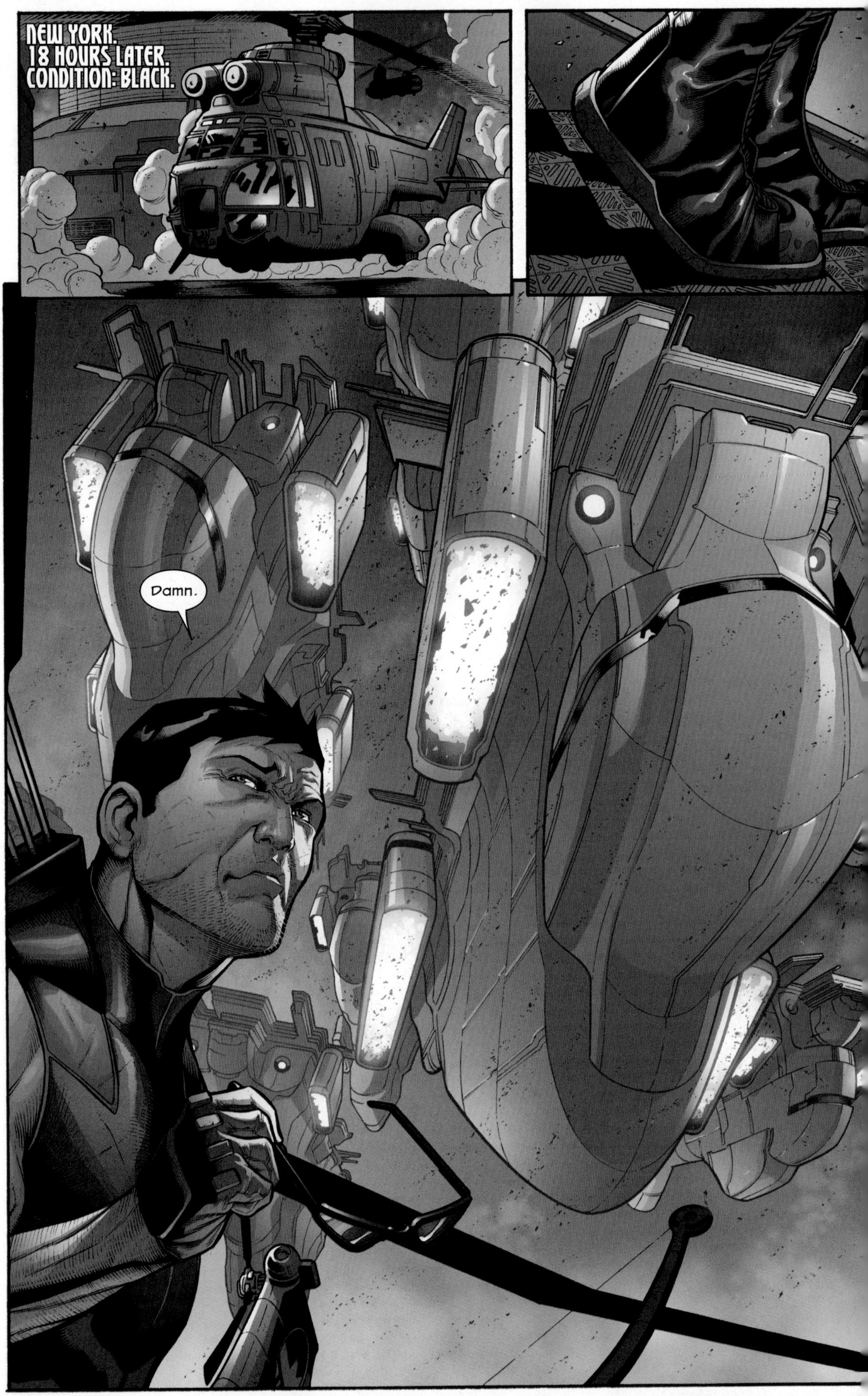
NEW YORK.
18 HOURS LATER.
CONDITION: BLACK.
Damn.

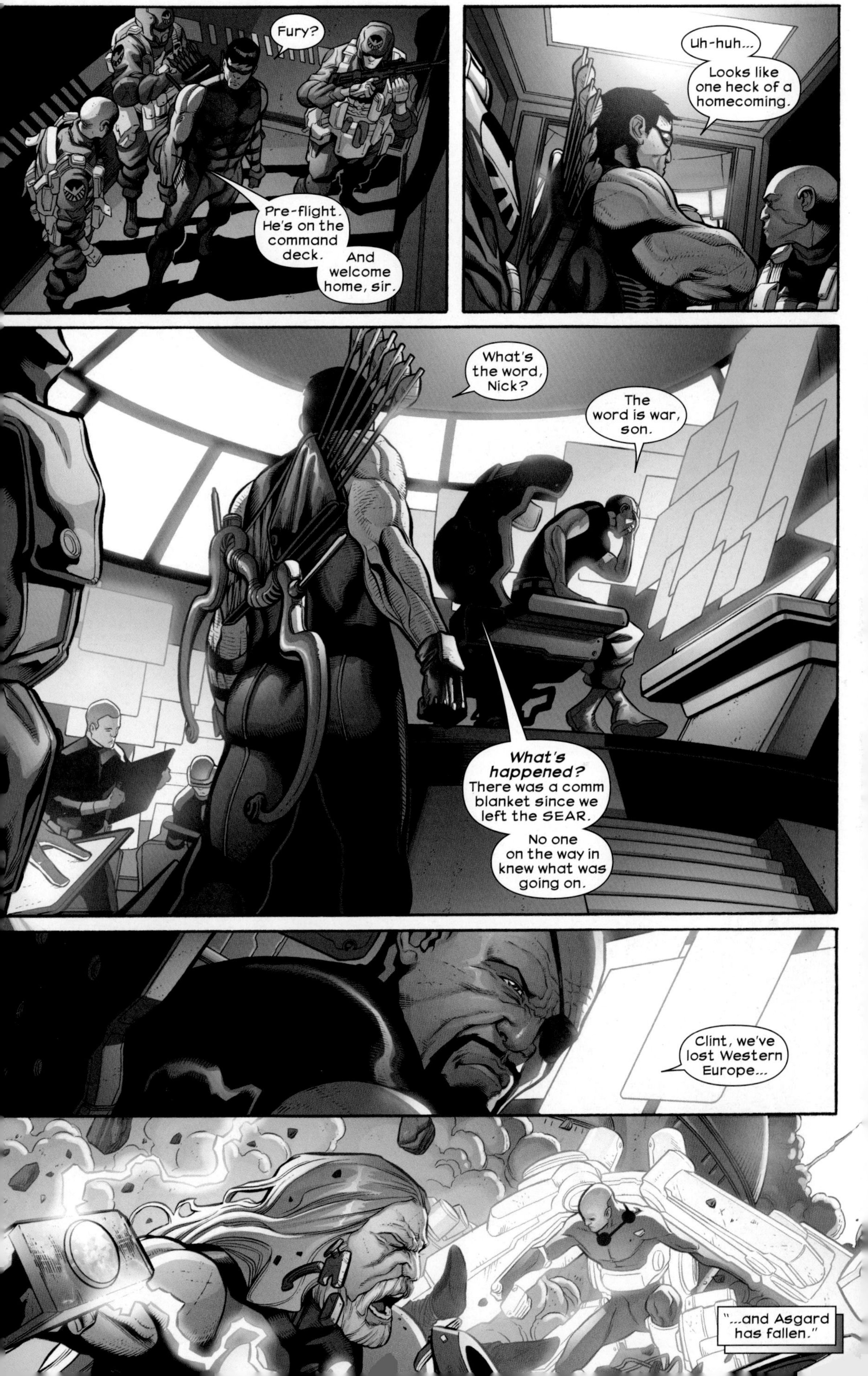
Fury?
Pre-flight. He's on the command deck.
And welcome home, sir.
Uh-huh...
Looks like one heck of a homecoming.
What's the word, Nick?
The word is war, son.
What's happened? There was a comm blanket since we left the SEAR.
No one on the way in knew what was going on.
Clint, we've lost Western Europe...
"...and Asgard has fallen."

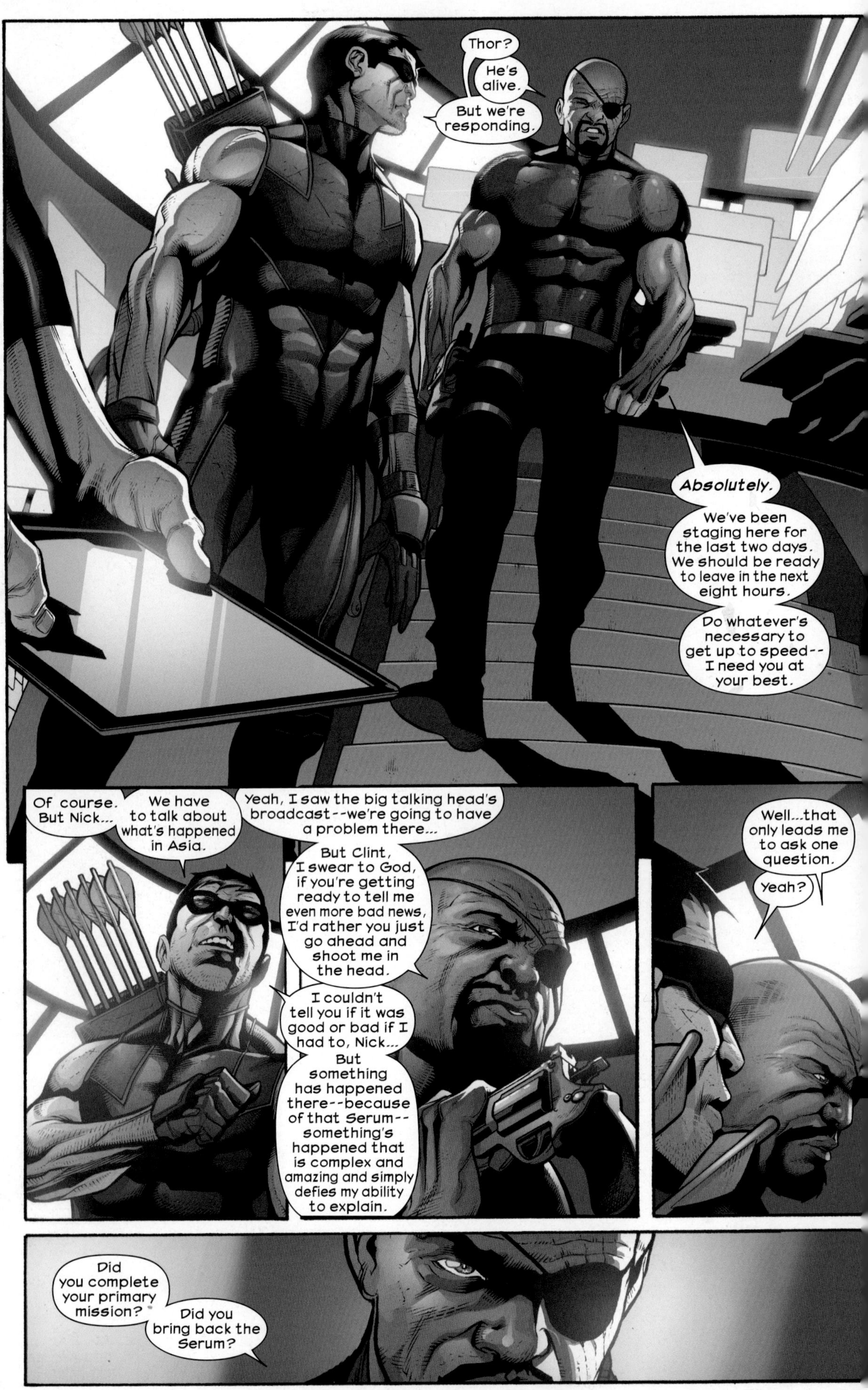
Thor?
He's alive.
But we're responding.
Absolutely.
We've been staging here for the last two days. We should be ready to leave in the next eight hours.
Do whatever's necessary to get up to speed-- I need you at your best.
Of course. But Nick...
We have to talk about what's happened in Asia.
Yeah, I saw the big talking head's broadcast--we're going to have a problem there...
But Clint, I swear to God, if you're getting ready to tell me even more bad news, I'd rather you just go ahead and shoot me in the head.
I couldn't tell you if it was good or bad if I had to, Nick...
But something has happened there--because of that Serum--something's happened that is complex and amazing and simply defies my ability to explain.
Well...that only leads me to ask one question.
Yeah?
Did you complete your primary mission?
Did you bring back the Serum?

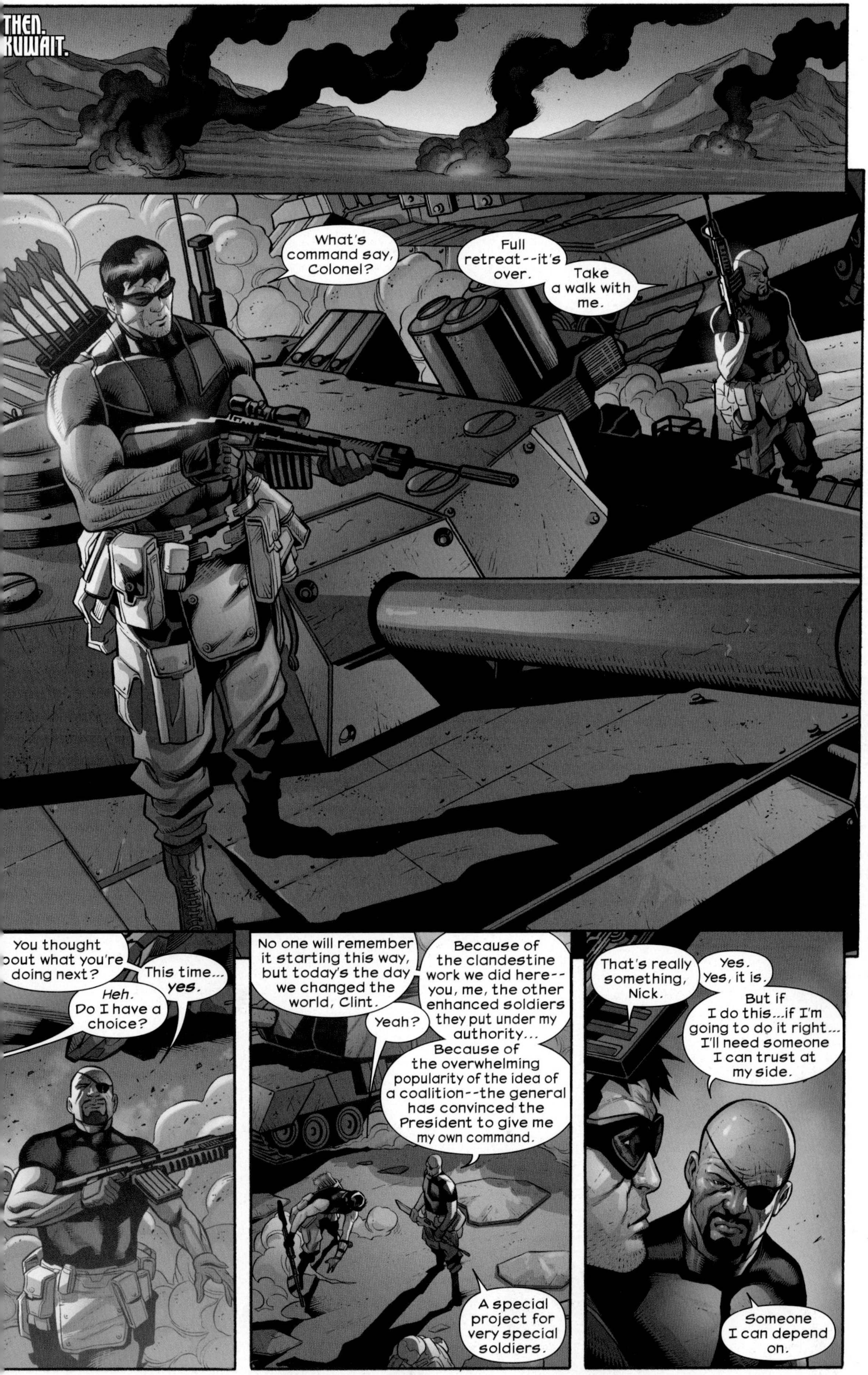
THEN.
KUWAIT.
What's command say, Colonel?
Full retreat--it's over.
Take a walk with me.
You thought bout what you're doing next?
Heh. Do I have a choice?
This time... *yes.*
No one will remember it starting this way, but today's the day we changed the world, Clint.
Yeah?
Because of the clandestine work we did here--you, me, the other enhanced soldiers they put under my authority...
Because of the overwhelming popularity of the idea of a coalition--the general has convinced the President to give me my own command.
A special project for very special soldiers.
That's really something, Nick.
Yes. Yes, it is.
But if I do this...if I'm going to do it right... I'll need someone I can trust at my side.
Someone I can depend on.

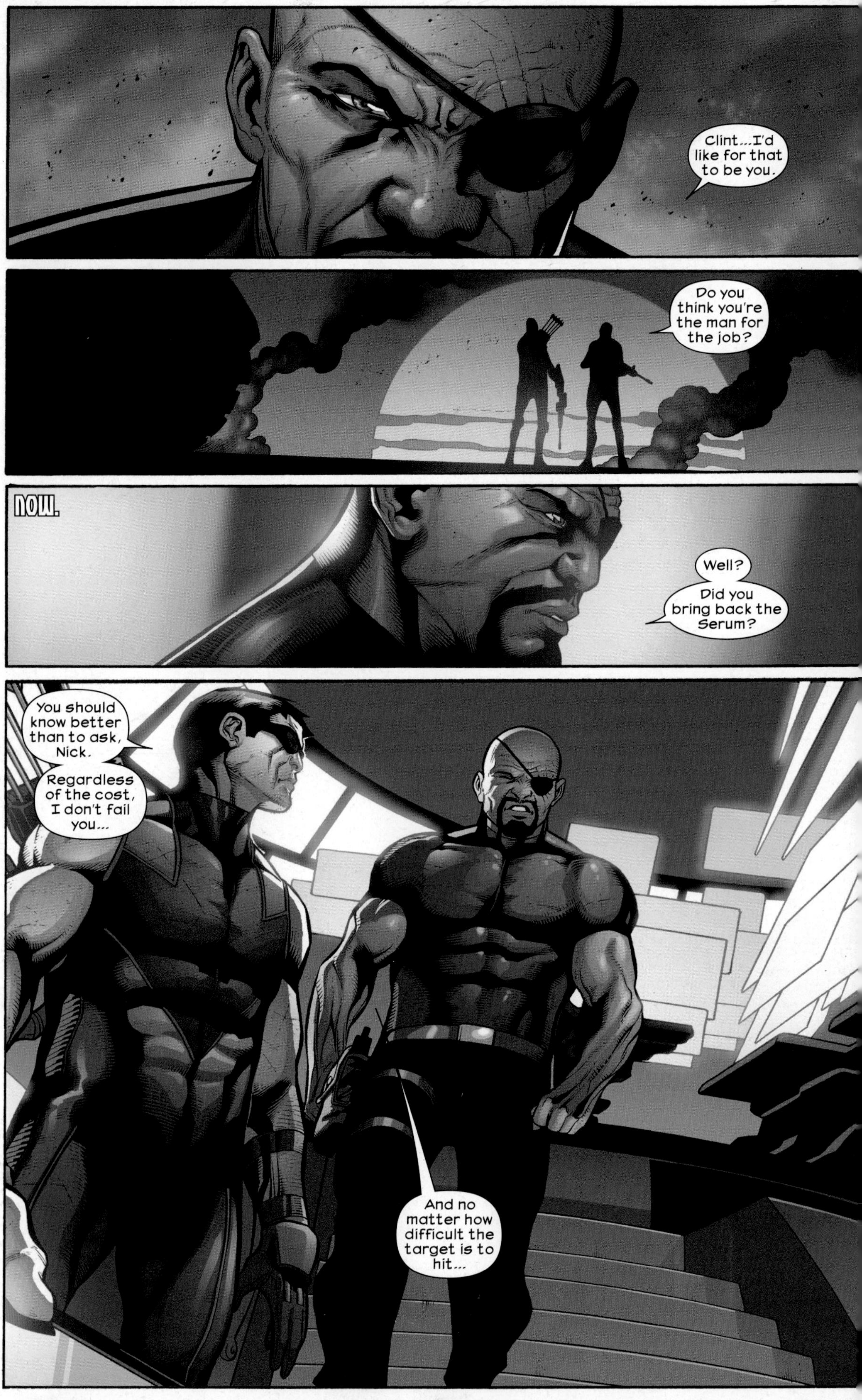
Clint...I'd like for that to be you.
Do you think you're the man for the job?
NOW.
Well?
Did you bring back the Serum?
You should know better than to ask, Nick.
Regardless of the cost, I don't fail you...
And no matter how difficult the target is to hit...

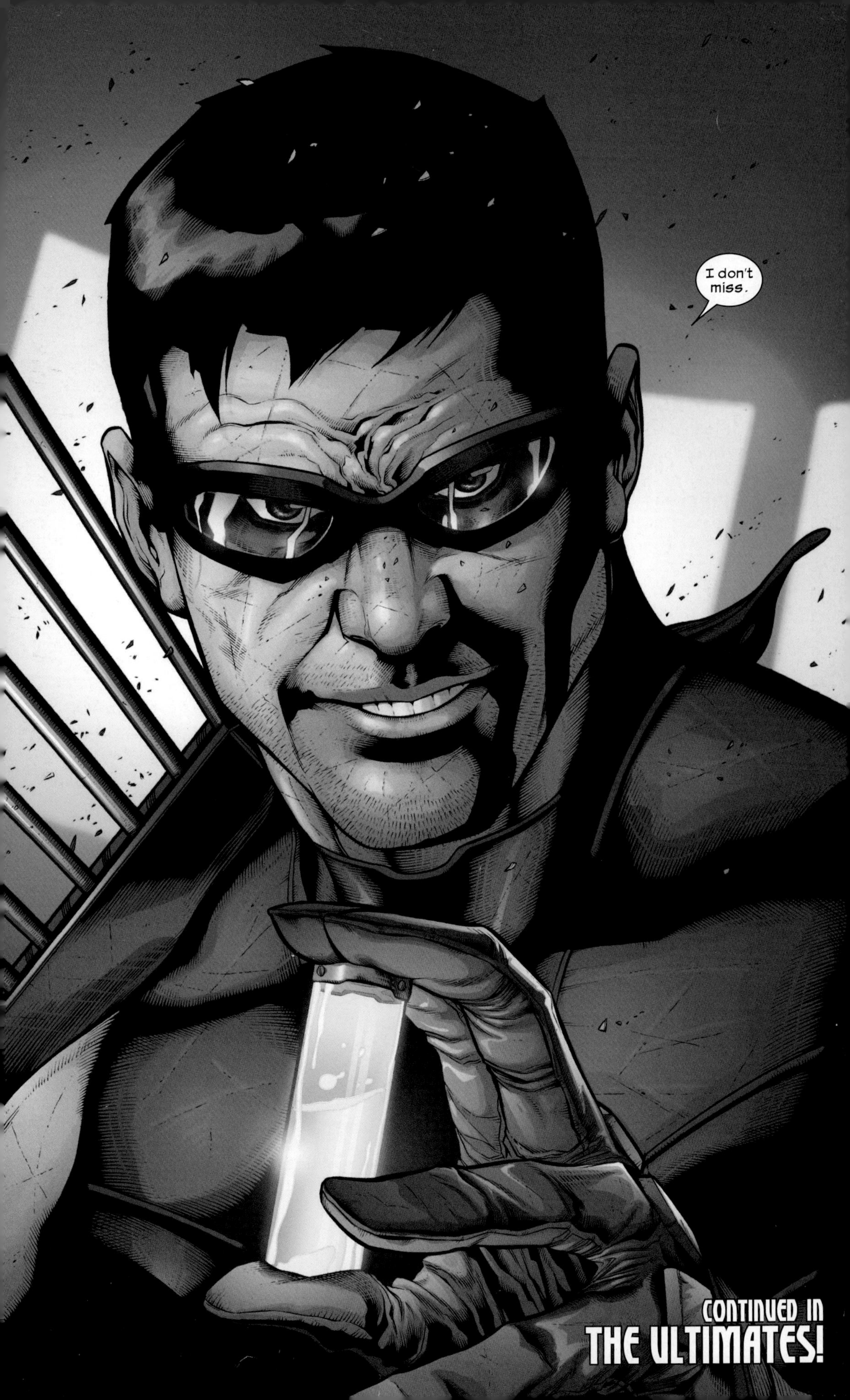
I don't miss.
CONTINUED IN
THE ULTIMATES!

ULTIMATE COMICS HAWKEYE #1

Script by JONATHAN HICKMAN
Art by RAFA SANDOVAL & JORDI TARRAGONA

Rafa, so excited to be working with you! I know that you will absolutely kill this, so just let loose and do what feels natural and this will turn out great. A couple things before we get started:

1. Please take what is written in this document merely as a suggestion of how things should be laid out. If you have a better idea for how things should be designed, or how to approach a specific shot, PLEASE... do that! All I ask is that you respect specific beats if they are delineated.

2. While there will be talky bits, you should definitely think of this mini as more of an action movie. This is Hawkeye -- he DOES things -- so, while I'll be trying to set you up accordingly... if you feel like I'm losing track of that, let's course-correct.

Beyond that, if you have any questions, or want to talk things over, please feel free to contact me whenever you want.

Here we go...

Page 1 - (3 panels)

Panel 1 - A helicopter landing on the flight deck of a Triskelion base that is located on an extended, artificial outcropping directly connected to an industrialized mainland. NOT NEW YORK... BANGKOK. This is the capital city of the SEAR.

NOTE: The name may change, but SEAR is the Southeast Asian Republic. It is comprised of the countries that currently make up the Indochina peninsula: Cambodia, Laos, Vietnam, Thailand, Singapore and Myanmar.

NOTE: All of this is a stand in for China, which we want to somewhat ape the visual style of (So we have concocted a 'new BIG country'). The point here is that this Triskelion should have been sitting in front of HONG KONG, and since we still want that vibe... let's go with a jacked-up BANGKOK.

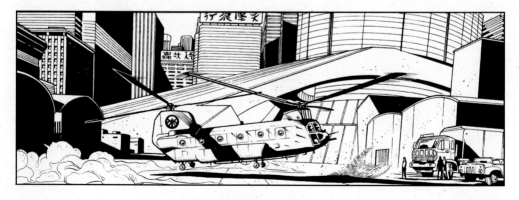

CAPTION

The Triskelion
Bangkok.
The SEAR

CAPTION

Condition: ORANGE.

Panel 2 - HAWKEYE, Clint Barton, walking towards us after getting out of the Helicopter. A few steps behind him is a junior officer that is carrying his bags (which contains his bow and arrows, uniform and other various badass equipment). A base Captain approaches him -- filling him in on what has been going on while he was in transit.

NOTE: Clint -- and everyone else on the Triskelion -- is outfitted in military dress (We'll get him in costume at the end of the issue).

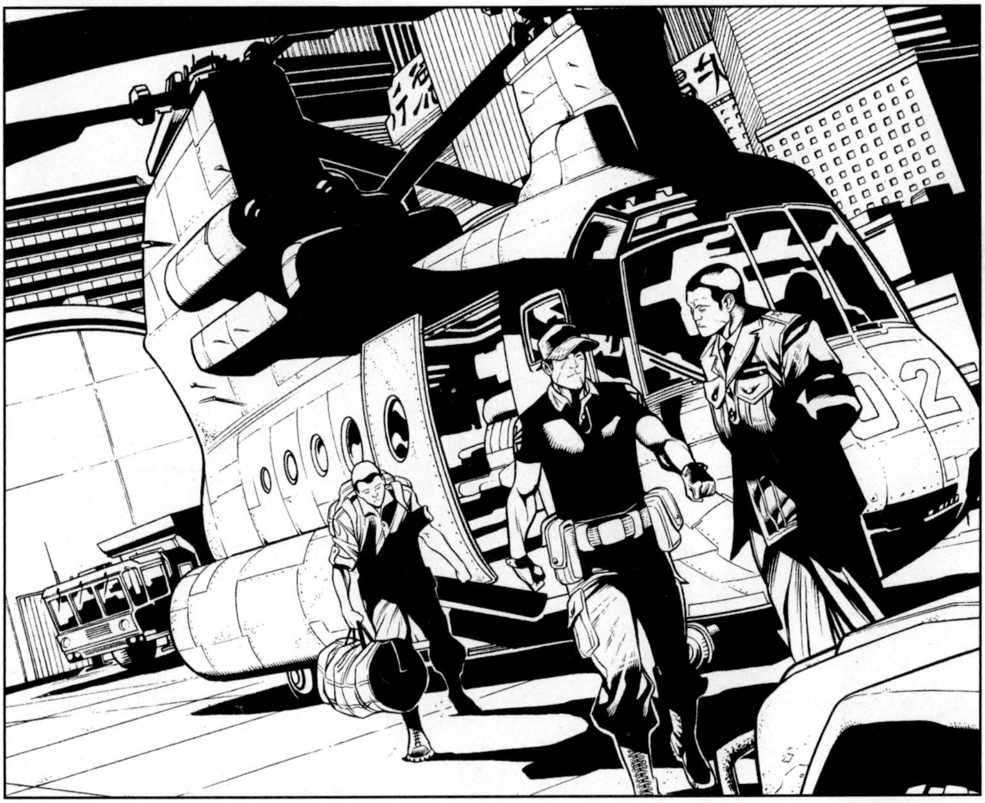

HAWKEYE

Let's hear it, soldier.

CAPTAIN

Fighting broke out less than an hour ago.

The SEAR government insists that the rebels only control a small portion of the capital, but our intel from various safe houses inside the city say otherwise. We're currently re-tasking Satellites to get a better look.

The SEAR are mobilizing their armed forces now, but, as per our existing treaties, the import of various monied interests and other general humpty-dump, they would appreciate it if our vast experience in population control was on stand-by should they need our assistance.

                                HAWKEYE
            Oh, it's just gonna be a lovely day, isn't it?
                                CAPTAIN
            We also had two SEAR state scientists -- confirmed
            as a geneticist and a weaponeer -- show up seeking
            asylum just as the fighting broke out.

Panel 3 - Closer on the three as they are getting ready to enter the
Triskelion. Hawkeye looks back over his shoulder (Across the bay
towards Bangkok).

                                HAWKEYE
            Anything else?
                                CAPTAIN
            General Fury politely requested that you contact
            him immediately when you reach Op Central.
                                HAWKEYE
            Well, I don't know what the rush is...

Page 2 - (5 panels)
Panel 1 - BIG PANEL. A large, somewhat overhead, establishing shot
of the Triskelion and Bangkok behind it. A Helicarrier hovers
in the air -- positioned in between the base and the city which
appears, from the ominous plumes of smoke coming from its innards,
to be on fire in several places.

                                HAWKEYE
            ...It's not like the world is on fire or anything.

Panel 2 - Clint walks into a VERY busy OPs room. People are scurrying
everywhere. No one should looked panicked, these are professionals,
they look determined.

Ops Central.

Panel 3 - In the foreground, Clint and the OPs chief (Think of him
as something like the base commander -- middle-aged and worthy of
respect) are at an ID station. In the background, is a giant monitor
displaying a map of the SEAR (Leave the monitor blank -- we'll
fill that in with a display map explaining the makeup of this new
country).

Hawkeye should be putting his hand on a scanning device.

OPS CHIEF
Identification and voice authorization, sir.
HAWKEYE
Barton, Clint. 253519987
ID: HAWKEYE.

SFX
Be-doop!
HAWKEYE
Get General Fury on the line.

Page 3 - (6 PANELS)
NOTE: Rafa, one bigger panel (1/3 of the page at the top, the other
5 take up the bottom 2/3s). And a little dense here, so talking-
talking at the bottom of the page.
    Panel 1 - Looking past Hawkeye and the Ops Chief at the giant
monitor showing the map of the SEAR (again leave this blank, Rafa).

HAWKEYE
Show me what we've got, chief.
OPS CHIEF
Five intelligence hubs operating inside of
Bangkok. Lotsa good data from there, but as we move
deeper into SEAR territory our reliability breaks
down fairly quickly.
    Which is why, when I say we think all this
started outside the capital... it sure ain't with
much confidence.
    We also...
COMM OFFICER
(interrupting)
CHIEF!

Panel 2 - On a communications officer (he should have a futuristic
headset/comm-device thing) manning a workstation. He looks over
towards us and says...

COMM OFFICER
I've got the General.
Putting him on the big board.

Panel 3 - Nick Fury's face now dominates the large monitor. Hawkeye, with his back to us, stands in front of it.

HAWKEYE
Boss.
FURY
Clint.
    I'm pretty sure I sent you over there to make sure things DID NOT go to hell.

Panel 4 - Hawkeye. A smirk.
HAWKEYE
Nick, I swear... she was already pregnant.
            (tail)
Do we have anything official yet?

Panel 5 - On Fury, back in his command center at the New York Triskelion.

FURY
Yes we do.
    The United States government has received a formal request from the Chancellor of the SEAR asking us to assist in the domestic peacekeeping efforts already underway.
    Consider this a go order.

Panel 6 - On Hawkeye and the Ops chief. The chief saying this in Clint's ear... He doesn't want to interrupt the conversation between his two superiors with a status update.

                    HAWKEYE
        You've got to be kidding me.
                     FURY
              (off panel/from the monitor)
        If only... just got off the phone with the
        President.
                   OPS CHIEF
                  (small)
        The Helicarrier is being deployed, sir.

        It'll be in overwatch in five minutes.
                    HAWKEYE
        You want to stay on the line for this, Nick?

Page 4 - (5 PANELS)
Panel 1 - With the monitor behind him, Clint recoils from a massive explosion happening outside the Triskelion lighting up the room.
    NOTE: Maybe the transmission is breaking up from Fury.

                    FURY
        Yes, I...
                     SFX
        BA-BOOOOOOM!
                   HAWKEYE
        What the....

Panel 2 - Exterior shot. We see a chunk, in the center of the Helicarrier, blowing apart from an explosion. It begins to break in half.

                 NO DIALOGUE

Panel 3 - Back inside the Triskelion. Clint and the others looking out the window.

HAWKEYE

    Alert One, chief.
      Scramble secondary responders.

Panel 4 - On a super-being (in what would be consider normal,
COMMON, Asian attire... uhhhhhh, think AKIRA, I guess), with
his arms spread wide (like he's pulling it apart). He floats in
between two huge pieces of the Helicarrier. It should almost be
like an exploded diagram at the edges... As if this super-being is
literally deconstructing the ship into parts.

NO DIALOGUE

Panel 5 - On the chief, yelling into Clint's ear. Clint ignores him
as he eyeballs the attacker outside the window.

HAWKEYE

    I've got him.
      Have an assault team meet me on the roof!

OPS CHIEF

There's more than one out there!

HAWKEYE

    Wha...

Page 5 - (4 PANELS)
Panel 1 - The top of the Triskelion explodes.

SFX

BOOOOOM!

Panel 2 - Our original super-being has been joined by two more
(one has glowing eyes and is the one that just caused part of
the building to blow, the other has like a holographic, clawed
guantlets). The three of them are hovering outside the now-
shattered upper section of the Triskelion. Both should be dressed
similarly to the original one -- all three are male.

NO DIALOGUE

Panel 3 - Hawkeye, looking back, over his shoulder... his eyes wide
at what he sees. He's in the middle of a now destroyed -- and OPEN to
the exterior -- Ops Center.

NO DIALOGUE

Panel 3 - A black panel.

NO DIALOGUE

Page 6 - (5 panels)
NOTE: THE NEXT EIGHT PAGES ARE A FLASHBACK!

Panel 1 - A black panel.

CAPTION
    It starts with a cough.

Panel 2 - Close on the Chancellor of SEAR. He looks up at us while
taking off his glasses, as if to make sure he has heard correctly.

CAPTION
    One month ago.
    Bangkok.
    The SEAR.
    The Chancellor's State Room.
                        CAPTION
    Condition: YELLOW.
                    CHANCELLOR
    Excuse me?

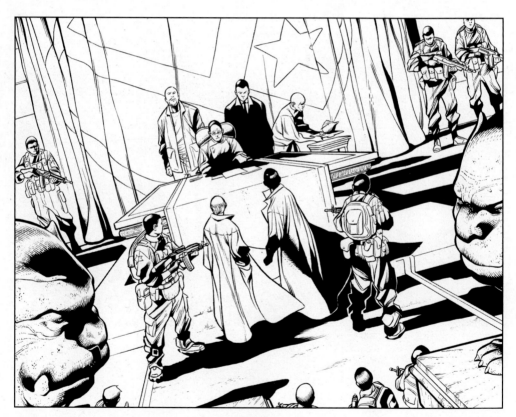

Panel 3 - A wide, establishing shot. We are in a great hall. Two
scientists, DR. LEUNG (old) and DR. ZHENG (young)(and along with
them, TWO accompanying guards [ready to shoot them should they
act up]), stand before, and below, a dais on which sits a large
horizontal table. Seated at this table are the Chancellor (in what
is clearly some type of ceremonial Military garb), and an underling

on each side of him (One dressed as a civilian, and the other a businessperson). Behind them, on the wall, is an absolutely massive ornamental version of the SEAR national symbol. Soldiers line the width of the room, except behind the Chancellor... that dude is a waiter/assistant/butler type.

                              DR. LEUNG
          A cough, Chancellor.
                              (tail)
          It's the first visible sign of infection.
                              DR. ZHENG
          This is followed by a low-grade fever until the
          virus has completed its cycle.

Panel 4 - On the Chancellor and his two flunkies - they look like someone #@$%ed in their tea.

                              FLUNKIE ONE
          That sounds...
                              CHANCELLOR
          Unremarkable.

Panel 4 - A medium shot of the Doctors - Explaining THE PLAN. Zheng looks arrogant, Leung, apologetic for his partner... cutting his eyes over at him as he apologizes for his rudeness.
                              DR. ZHENG
          Well... that's the point, sir.
                              DR. LEUNG
          Excuse me, Chancellor. Forgive us...
              What my colleague means is that if the reaction
          was too severe then it's possible quarantine
          protocols could be enacted...
              Thereby stunting the effectiveness of what we
          are calling... the PLAN.

Page 7 - (5 panels)
Panel 1 - On the Chancellor. Someone behind him is setting tea in front of him. HE IS NOT LOOKING AT THE DOCTORS, BUT SEEMS DECIDEDLY UNHAPPY.

                              NO DIALOGUE

Panel 2 - The Chancellor takes a sip. STILL NOT LOOKING.

NO DIALOGUE

Panel 3 - The two doctors watch closely. Leung extremely nervous.

NO DIALOGUE

Panel 4 - The Chancellor puts down his cup. THE VERY BAREST OF LOOKS AT THE DOCTORS (AT US).

CHANCELLOR

Continue.

Panel 5 - On the two Doctors.

DR. ZHENG

It consists of two parts.

DR. LEUNG

The Plan.

DR. ZHENG

Yes. The Plan has two parts.

DR. LEUNG

The first, is THE VIRUS -- what we were already telling you about...

Page 8 - (4 PANELS)
Panel 1 - Our two doctors. Working in a high-tech, experimental, biological lab... but the kind of thing you'd never see depicted in a similar western setting. SO, yes, while this should be super-clean, orderly, and sterile, there's one thing should seem very out of order. WHERE THERE WOULD NORMALLY BE TEST ANIMALS, WE SHOULD SEE HUMANS.

CAPTION

It was created to fill certain criteria: The virus should be airborne. As we've already stated, it should produce minimal reactions. It should have a short incubation period and an extended infectious cycle. Also, for what it is, the virus should be durable and resistant to evolving from generation to generation.

Panel 2 - On a regular guy (dressed in a way that we will easily be able to follow him through the next three panels), getting a shot from an official looking SEAR dude. Soldiers with machine guns in the background.

CAPTION

Our plan to spread the Virus is to disguise it as required inoculations for tourists planning to leave the country. To produce the volume necessary we have been quietly creating multiple travel agencies that specialize in corporate packages. Things like end-of-the-year vacation bonuses and special prizes recognizing years of loyal service.

Panel 3 - A dense, crowded airport. Our guy walking through it.

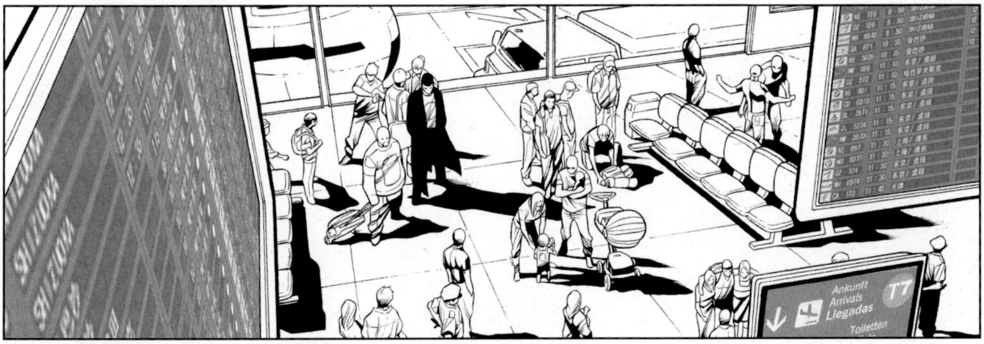
T7
Ankunft
Arrivals
Llegadas
Toiletten

CAPTION

We coordinated all of the vacations to originate within roughly the same 24 hour period of time and have pre-purchased roughly one-quarter to one-third of all flights departing from our central hub and connecting with the ten busiest airports throughout Asia and India. From there, our group split into ever increasingly smaller groups until only a couple or even a single individual reaches their final destination.

Panel 4 - The passenger section of a plane. It's a full flight. Our guy coughing into his hand.

CAPTION

Our testing shows that a single tainted person is enough to infect an entire plane within a thirty minute window. Our projections show 96 percent global contamination rate in ten days, and within one month the virus will have completed its predetermined task:

CAPTION

The complete rewriting of the human DNA code to deny the acceptance, adaptation and existence of an X Gene.

Page 9 - (5 PANELS)

Panel 1 - On the Chancellor. Eyebrow raised.

> **CHANCELLOR**
> Complete eradication?
> Forever?

Panel 2 - On the two doctors (mostly Leung). Very matter-of-fact.
Dr. Leung says...

> **DR. LEUNG**
> That's correct, Chancellor...
> (tail)
> No more mutants.

Panel 3 - On Dr. Zheng. While he's talking, he pulls out a small
rectangular case from his inside coat pocket.

> **DR. ZHENG**
> Of course, if this was the sole desired outcome
> of the PLAN, the entire endeavour would be quite
> pointless.
> While the acceptance of the X gene remains a
> random, unpredictable variable, the population
> advantages existing in the East remain valid.
> (tail)
> We simply have more people which should
> statistically produce more mutants.

Panel 4 - In a formal fashion, he opens up the case and presents
it to the senior member of the team, Dr. Leung... with experience,
come the honors.

> **DR. ZHENG**
> But in an arms race, mutually assured destruction
> simply means a prolonged stalemate...
> (tail)
> TO WIN, we must not only eliminate all of their
> weapons, but create new ones for ourselves.
> **DR. LEUNG**
> Which leads to the second part of The Plan...

Panel 5 - In the foreground, Dr. Leung, holds up/shows us a wicked-

looking syringe. In the background, Dr. Zheng turns to one of the guards and gives him his cue.

> ### DR. LEUNG
> Chancellor, this is The SERUM.
> ### DR. ZHENG
> > (quietly)
> Bring in the test subject.

Page 10 - (5 PANELS)
Panel 1 - A wider shot of the room as several guards bring in a test subject (I'll leave it up to you on which way to go here, Rafa -- either a brute or frail individual). They are maneuvering him (and let's do make it a guy) by these long poles that are connected to a collar around his neck -- like he's an animal or something.

> ### PRISONER
> <Let me go!>
> > <PLEASE!... I haven't done anything wrong.>

Panel 2 - The Chancellor. One eyebrow raised.

> ### CHANCELLOR
> What is <u>THIS?</u>

Panel 3 - Dr. Zheng explains. In the background, Dr. Leung prepares to inject the subject.

> ### DR. ZHENG
> Something different. Something better than the X gene. Something... new.
> > And what emerges we call THE PEOPLE.

Panel 4 - The needle. Piercing the skin.

DR. LEUNG

Just a pinch now.

Panel 5 - The subject has an immediate response. Boils pop up all over his body. He screams in pain.

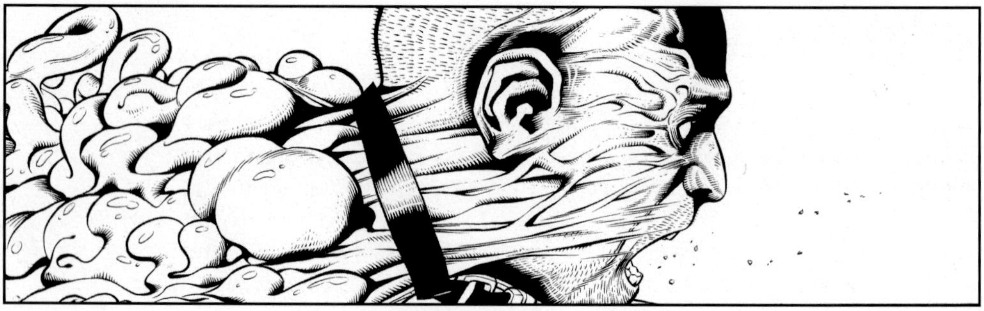

PRISONER

AAAAAARRRRRRGGGGHHHHHH!!!!!

Page 11 - (3 PANELS)

Panel 1 - On the Doctors looking on. Their mouths open in wonder. Behind them we see the Chancellor and his companions doing the same.

DR. ZHENG

It's something, isn't it?

CHANCELLOR

My god...

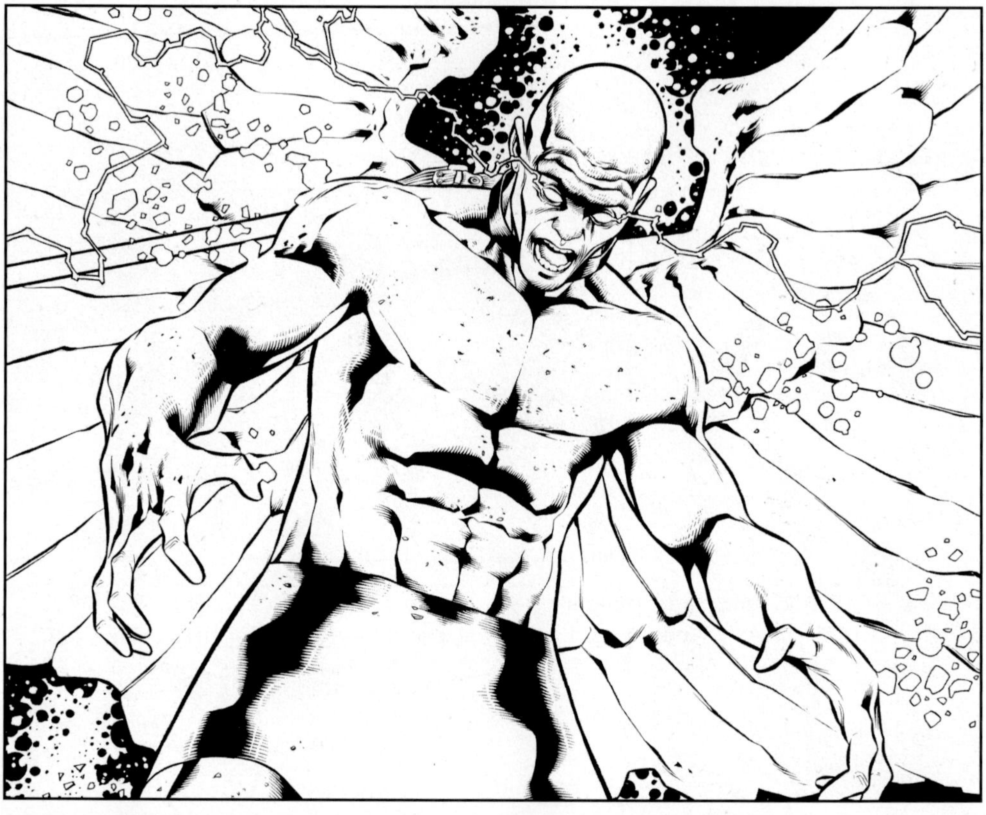

Panel 2 - On our transformed subject (he should still be tethered around his neck). Rafa, this guy should look like the most amazing fanboy superhero ever. He should have that starfield effect where any shadows would be, kirby-crackle and maybe wings... you get the idea... He looks off in kind of a daze as not only has his physical body been transformed, but also his mind... He says...

PRISONER

Ohhhh...
    I see it now -- the stairs of creation, the emergence of a second skin... I ascend and float above everything...
    There on the horizon, Tu'an. And beyond, beyond the chaos that comes from the sun searing away the night, beyond the death deserved by those that bring the change... the dome.
(tail)
There will be a breaking of the old order. It cannot be stopped.
    I can see it.

Panel 3 - On Dr. Zheng and the guards. Zheng motions for them to act.

DR. ZHENG

    That's quite enough...

Page 12 - (4 PANELS)
Panel 1 - On the guards firing their machine guns -- DO NOT SHOW the subject being shot... this is much stronger if we just imply it.

SFX

    BLAM!
    BLAM!
    BLAM!

Panel 2 - Back on the Doctors talking to the Chancellor. In the background, the Guards are firing a couple of extra bullets into the prone body of the subject... just to be sure.
SFX

    BLAM!
    BLAM!

DR. LEUNG

What was that... Temporal vision?

DR. ZHENG

Maybe... or possibly some kind of empathetic
precognition?

DR. LEUNG

Regardless Chancellor, each of our twenty-three
subjects we've tested the serum on have manifested
a significantly different powerset.
(tail)
It appears as if the PEOPLE are both formidable
and diverse.

Panel 3 - On the Chancellor and his Flunkies. One of the flunkies
leans over to whisper to him.

FLUNKY
(very small)
A paradigm shift.

CHANCELLOR

And are you sure that only WE have this?

Panel 4 - On Dr. Zheng.

DR. ZHENG

The squeamish nature of the western powers has
made them hesitant to aggressively enter the
arena of genetic engineering -- we share no such
deficiency.
Chancellor...Our mastery of the field is
unmatched.

Page 13 - (6 PANELS)
Panel 1 - In profile, the Chancellor and the Doctors. Him looking
down at them.

CHANCELLOR

And how would you choose who receives the serum?
We would have to be particular.

DR. LEUNG

Of course... we have already targeted an initial

group, Chancellor, made up of only dedicated
nationalists.

                    DR. ZHENG
And beyond that, we have also began additional...
conditioning.

                    CHANCELLOR
How many?

Panel 2 - Dr. Leung. Matter-of-fact.

                    DR. LEUNG
    Just over one hundred thousand.

Panel 3 - On the Chancellor and his Flunkies. Smiling like cats who
just ate canaries.

                    NO DIALOGUE

Panel 4 - Close on the Chancellor. Leaning forward just to be
clear...

                    CHANCELLOR
    Then, if we want, the world is ours.
                        (tail)
    Such great power...
        Can something like that truly be contained?

Panel 5 - On Dr. Zheng. Famous last words...

                    DR. ZHENG
    Put any fears you have to rest, Chancellor...
        I promise... We can control them.

Page 14 - (4 PANELS)
NOTE: Back in the present, with the three super-beings (Now we know
that these are THE PEOPLE) attacking the Triskelion.
    Not so controlled...
Panel 1 - BIG PANEL. On the PEOPLE attacking the base. One is
shooting beams out of his eyes, blasting away at the SHIELD
troops within. The one with holographic claws is jumping into the
Triskelion Ops center. The last one who has magnetic powers hovers
behind the others.

CAPTION

The Triskelion
Bangkok.
The SEAR

CAPTION

Condition: RED.

Panel 2 – Three SHIELD agents show up with assault rifles
preparing to fire on the PEOPLE.

SHIELD AGENTS

Everybody DOWN!

Panel 3 – The one with magnetic powers causes the assault rifles to
be snatched out of the SHIELD agent's hands.

SHIELD AGENTS

Wha...?

Panel 4 – He turns the rifles on everyone else in the room.

Unloading. SHIELD Agents are falling everywhere.

SHIELD AGENTS

AARRRGGGGH!

Page 15 - (5 PANELS)

Panel 1 - Hawkeye ducks down as an upright, giant, glass strategy board beside him is being shot at... IT SHATTERS.

NO DIALOGUE

Panel 2 - On Hawkeye's hands, picking up two pieces of the broken glass.

HAWKEYE

That's it....
Shoot at the guy who can turn anything into a weapon -- MISS, and hit a bunch of glass...

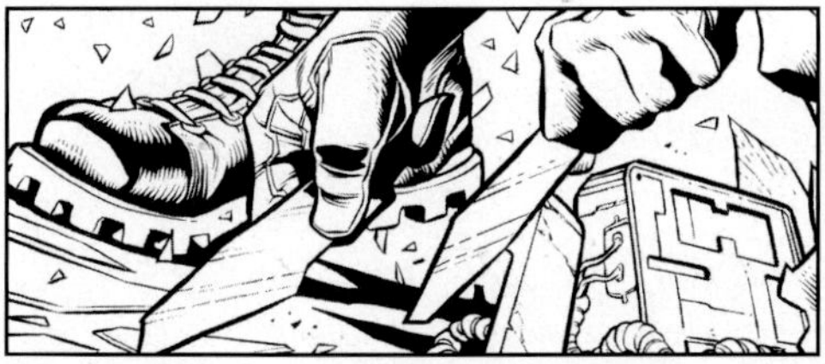

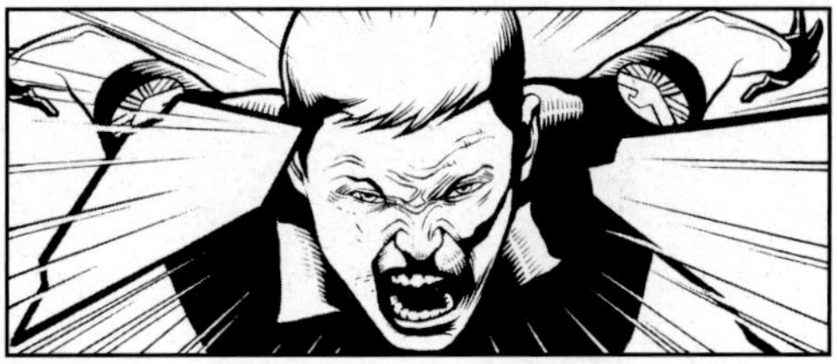

Panel 3 - He throws the two pieces of broken glass right at us.

HAWKEYE

Brilliant.

Panel 4 - The Magnetic powered of the PEOPLE snaps back as he gets hit by the shards of glass -- he dies immediately. Beside him, the one with the laser eyes looks back as his companion falls (his eyes bleeding energy).

MAGNETIC

UUKK!

Panel 5 - Very close on Laser Eyes... NOT HAPPY.

NO DIALOGUE

Page 16 - (5 PANELS)

Panel 1 - He shoots the beam out of his eyes, aiming at Clint, who is flipping and pirouetting out of the way. In the background, the junior officer who had Clint's bags on the opening page is moving into the room... he's got Clint's bow (note, the bow should have the arrows attached to it).

OFFICER

HAWKEYE!

Panel 2 - He throws him the bow -- Clint dives towards it. Almost touching already.

OFFICER

CATCH!

Panel 3 - Clint catches and fires it as he's falling to the ground.

NO DIALOGUE

Panel 4 - Clint, in the background, on the floor having just fired the arrow. In the foreground, Laser Eyes falls backwards dead... the arrow tagging him in the forehead.

NO DIALOGUE

Panel 5 - Clint, whipping his head around... only one of the PEOPLE left, and there's something going on behind him.

CLAWS
(off panel)

<Stay back!>

Page 17 - (5 PANELS)
Panel 1 - Wide. We can see that the last of THE PEOPLE has taken a hostage and is surrounded by SHIELD agents.

CLAWS

<STAY BACK OR HE DIES!>

Panel 2 - Hawkeye pushing through everyone surrounding the last of the PEOPLE and the SHIELD agent. He brushes past the Ops Chief.

OPS CHIEF

Let him go or we don't have anything to talk about... Let him go now!

HAWKEYE

Easy, Chief...

Panel 3 - On Hawkeye, Claws and the captured SHIELD agent.

CLAWS

<STAY! BACK!>

SHIELD AGENT

Oh god... he's going to kill me.

HAWKEYE

Son, look at me...

Panel 4 - On Hawkeye, His bow slightly raised -- arrow nocked. Very calm while everyone else is freaking out.

HAWKEYE

I want you to relax. Everything is going to be fine. Do you know why?

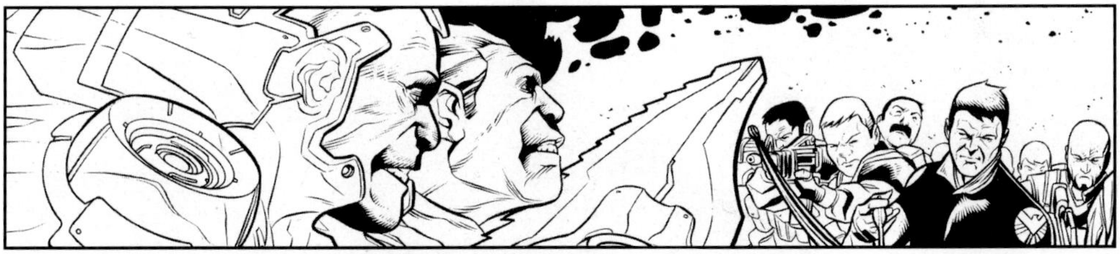

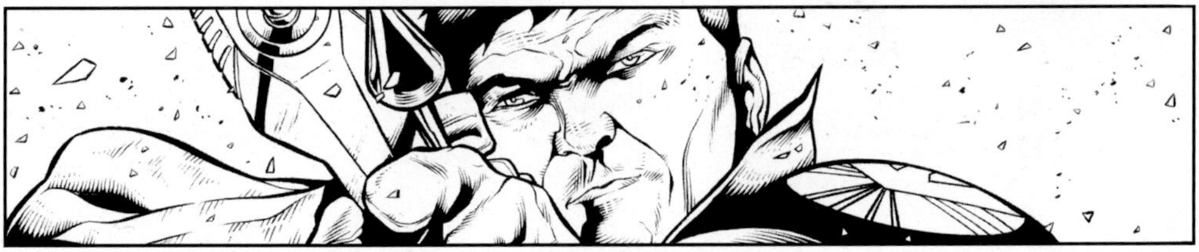

Panel 5 - On the last of the PEOPLE... Peaking his head around from behind the SHIELD officer that he is still holding in front of him, tight. The arm that he is not using to restrain the officer should be hologram-ed up in a menacing way.

SHIELD AGENT

(small)

Why?

Page 18 - (5 PANELS)

Panel 1 - Same as the previous panel, except the last of the PEOPLE has been shot in between the eyes and is falling backwards away from SHIELD officer. His claw flickering/fading/etc away.

SFX

THUK!

Panel 2 - On Hawkeye. Slightly lowering his bow... His fingers on the other hand still spread from releasing an arrow.
   A very, very bad man.

HAWKEYE

   I don't miss.

Panel 3 - Wide. Everyone trying to assess the damage. The Ops Chief and the Captain who walked Clint in are talking to him.

HAWKEYE

   Chief, let's get a report on our condition ASAP...
      And do whatever you need to do to get the General back on line.

OPS CHIEF

   I'll let you know as soon as we have him.

HAWKEYE

   Captain...

CAPTAIN

   Yes, sir?

Panel 4 - Close on Hawkeye.

HAWKEYE

   Please go fetch me those two scientists in holding that were looking for asylum...
      I think we need to have a word.

Panel 5 - Exterior shot. The Triskelion, broken... smoke streaming from the damaged top section.

NO DIALOGUE

Page 19 - (5 PANELS)
Panel 1 - Same shot as the last panel on the previous page, except now it's night and the Triskelion has stopped smoking.

CAPTION

   Later.

CAPTION

The Triskelion
Bangkok.
The SEAR

CAPTION

Condition: RED.

Panel 2 - On Nick Fury. #@$%ed off. In his command center... He HAS NOT had a good day.

FURY

You want to run that by me again?

Panel 3 - BIG PANEL. On Hawkeye. NOW IN UNIFORM (This should be a design much like the first Hitch design used in ULTIMATES VOL. 1).

HAWKEYE

The SEAR government -- who we have an arms treaty with, and said treaty is the basis of why we have a base here -- has secretly neutered the world with a mutant eliminating virus and developed a weapons program that exceeds anything we've ever seen.

Panel 4 - Nick on a monitor as Hawkeye turns and looks at out two Doctors (Leung and Zheng) in the background guarded by SHIELD agents.

FURY

(from monitor)

And we got this from two of the scientists that worked on the program?

HAWKEYE

Yes, sir.

You want me to have them shot?

Panel 5 - On Fury in his Command Center. Clint on a monitor.

FURY

Not just yet.

Do we have any confirmation that these PEOPLE are, in fact, trying to overthrow the SEAR government?

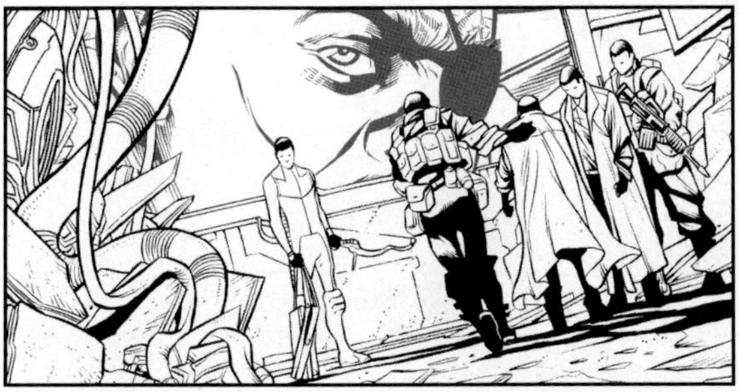

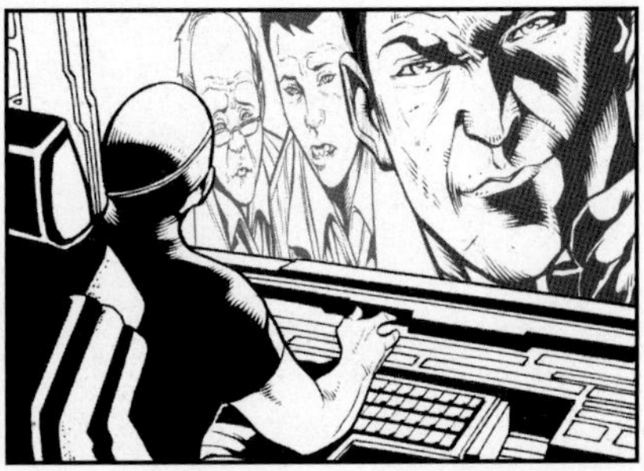

HAWKEYE

Nothing concrete, but it looks that way.

Page 20 - (3 PANELS)

Panel 1 - On Nick Fury. Rubbing his chin.

FURY

So now we're now behind in an arms race that we didn't even know about until today...

    Which is based on technology we don't understand and a process we don't possess.

(tail)

And right now, we don't have any idea who's going to end up with it.

Panel 2 - On Hawkeye.

HAWKEYE

Pretty much.

    What do you want me to do, Nick?

Panel 3 - BIG PANEL. On Nick Fury. Back in his command center. Leaning forward from his command chair...

FURY

What do you think, soldier...

(tail)

Go get me that serum.